Nick Bakay's
TALE OF THE TAPE

Nick Bakay's
TALE OF THE TAPE

by *Nick Bakay & Robin Bakay*

TAKING ON THE WORLD
OF SPORTS, ONE FIGHT AT A TIME

HYPERION
ESPN
BOOKS

Illustrated by Drew Friedman

Library of Congress Cataloging-in-Publication Data

Bakay, Nick.
    Nick Bakay's tale of the tape : taking on the world of sports, one fight at a time / Nick Bakay and Robin Bakay.
      p. cm.
    ISBN 0-7868-8879-2
    1. Sports—Miscellanea. 2. Sports—Humor. I. Title: Tale of the tape. II. Bakay, Robin. III. Title.
  GV707.B35   2004
796'.02—dc22   2003067687

Hyperion books are available for special promotions and premiums. For details contact Michael Rentas, Manager, Inventory and Premium Sales, Hyperion, 77 West 66th Street, 11th floor, New York, New York 10023, or call 212-456-0133.

Designed by Steve Polacek and produced by Jim Forni of SBI.Razorfish.

FIRST EDITION

10 9 8 7 6 5 4 3 2 1

ACKNOWLEDGMENTS

Nick: At ESPN, I owe an enormous debt of thanks to so many, in particular John Walsh, Vince D'Oria, Glenn Jacobs, Norby Williamson, Mark Preisler, Gary Belsky, Neil Fine, Mark Shapiro, Keith Olberman, Dan Patrick, Chris Berman, and Kenny Mayne, to name only a few. Special thanks to all who did the real work—the editors and producers who turned these things into TV—no small task.

Of course, I wouldn't be here without Allan Havey, Lucia Aparicio, and my mom, and this project wouldn't be here if not for Gretchen Young and Natalie Kaire at Hyperion, Lee Kernis, David Vigliano, Mike Harriot and the incomparable Drew Friedman.

Robin: I'd like to thank Veronica Abney, Miriam Myers, Glenn Jacobs, Mark Preisler, the cities of Las Vegas, New Orleans, New York, everyone in Hollywood who didn't shaft us, and last, but not least, a very special thanks to Eddie Gorodetsky for making us date in the first place.

CONFESSIONS OF A FIGHT FAN

I'm still haunted by the cover of a *U.S. News & World Report* I passed at a newsstand a while back: "*Americans are redefining their sense of hell.*"

My first thought: "Wait a minute, you can do that?!" Up until that moment, I had no idea "tweaking" damnation was an option. Silly me, needlessly locked into the rigid belief that hell is other people's children, a world of constant car alarms, and being forced to watch that infomercial where they wax a dude's back hair. I just assumed hell wouldn't come with an *à la carte* menu, then I realized I'm already living in a world where the national pastime tweaks itself with interleague play—what could be the harm in running some new ideas up Satan's tailpole and see who salutes 'em?

Sufficiently tantalized, I read on, only to discover that after all that buildup it turns out people are merely seeing hell as less fire and brimstone, more simple alienation from God. Talk about going *soft*. Listen, I'm as much for a *comfy* Hades as the next guy, but there has to be a better definition, and I've got it: Hell is not knowing the answer to the big question—the primordial one that's been slithering through the reptilian core of our brain stems since the dawn of man:

Who would win in a street fight?

When the dust settles, who's gonna be left standing? Could the Steel Curtain manhandle Lombardi's Packers? Could Aquaman open a can of whup-ass and pour it all over the Hulk...*on land*? Something deep inside us *just has to know.*

Alas, the big answers remain in the cold case file for a variety of reasons, including the NyQuil shooters that made you sleep through the 1992 AFC Wild Card Game. Or maybe because a celebrity in great need of a beating is not a ranked heavyweight, and therefore will never go toe to toe with Mike Tyson. Therein lies the tragedy of life, because most dream matchups are never realized...Or are they?

The Tale of the Tape is about filling the aching void by exploring matchups, declaring winners, and answering the unanswerable. Who elected me judge and jury? It's often referred to as "a calling." I had no more hand in this than Joan of Arc, but it's important work. If you don't believe me, crack open the sports section, jump over the police blotter headlines and the editorials written by men old enough to have banged Babe Didrikson, and take a look at the big advertisers:

Hair replacement
Strip clubs
Gambling touts
Penile dysfunction

In all fairness, many women read the sports section, but the ad sales guys don't target them, unless you count the ads for "Amateur Night" or anything to do with soccer. No, the sports section is like the little drawer in the night table of a man's soul. Sort of like a Robert Bly seminar with strippers, which begs the question, What the hell happened to us? There was a time when the ad space was devoted to tires, hardware stores, and, if you were lucky, the occasional clearance sale on hernia trusses, thrown in for spice. Now, thanks to Rafael Palmeiro's Viagra, the sports section comes with a prospectus and fourteen pages of potential side effects. I think John Facenda said it best:

Do you fear the force of the wind?
The slash of the rain?
Go face them, and fight them.
Be savage again.

We need to get back to the basics, and what's more basic than the side-by-side comparison that is *The Tale of the Tape*? Oft imitated, never replicated, I like to think of it as the Oklahoma drill with jokes. It's been a way of life for the past decade or so, and no one understands this better than my wife, Robin, who has written, punched, and edited hundreds of tales with me on cocktail napkins, turbulent in-flight table trays, lobster-stained Palm notepads, in the middle of a rewrite—wherever we were when the phone rang and we heard, "You got anything for the Sugar Bowl?" Too beautiful to be so gifted, she's the real reason I'm just living the dream.

But enough fumbling with the bra strap, let's get to the book. We've got the unexpurgated versions, and a bevy of brand-spanking-new ones, so unplug the phone, grab a ringside seat, chomp down on your mouth guard, and get ready for the best of the best as we proudly present *Nick Bakay's Tale of the Tape*.

Upsets? Plenty.
Jail poundings? You bet your sweet ass.
Ties? That's a push.

And away we go...

CONTENTS

CONTENTS

Icons

Who stacks up against the Babe? Aaron? Maguire? Bonds? I'll tell you who...Baby Ruth, the candy bar. Ruth put baseball on the map. What's the best thing you can say about the candy bar? It looks the same coming out as going in? The Babe versus the bar, a round-trip ticket versus a satisfyin' wallop of chewy caramel, let's see how they stack up at the Tale of the Tape...

LOOKS LIKE:
THE PLAYER: Ernest Borgnine
THE CANDY: Don't make me say it.
ADVANTAGE: Push...There are no winners here.

NICKNAME:
THE PLAYER: The Sultan of Swat
THE CANDY: The Czar of Nougat
ADVANTAGE: Push—either way it's a mouthful of trouble.

SECRET SHAME:
THE PLAYER: Constant drinking and whoring
THE CANDY: Slept with all three Musketeers.
ADVANTAGE: The candy!

SECRET OF SUCCESS:
THE PLAYER: Keep your eye on the ball.
THE CANDY: Xantham gum
ADVANTAGE: The player

Nick Bakay's Tale of the Tape

FEATURE FILM CAMEO:
THE PLAYER: *The Pride of the Yankees*
THE CANDY: A nude scene in
Caddyshack
X ADVANTAGE: The candy. It got more
laughs than Chevy Chase.

TOILET BOWL:
THE PLAYER: Huggin' it!
THE CANDY: Floatin' in it!
– – ADVANTAGE: Push—neither one sets a
good example for the kids!

STARTED CAREER AS:
THE PLAYER: A pitcher
THE CANDY: A nifty little shortstop
X ADVANTAGE: The player—you can never
get enough pitching.

NUT COUNT:
THE CANDY: Averages 23 nuts per bar.
THE PLAYER: 2
X ADVANTAGE: The player

IT IS SAID:
THE PLAYER: Hit a home run for a
sick kid.
THE CANDY: Used as a bribe for return
of Mesopotamian scrolls!
X ADVANTAGE: The candy

PAVED THE WAY FOR:
THE PLAYER: Reggie Jackson, the straw
that stirs the drink
THE CANDY: The Reggie bar, the snack
that stirs your colon
X ADVANTAGE: The candy, in a shocker

NEGOTIATIONS:
THE PLAYER: A slave to baseball's
monopoly
THE CANDY: An unrestricted *free* agent,
free to sell his services to any organi-
zation for half a buck
X ADVANTAGE: The candy bar!

SLOGAN:
THE PLAYER: "Who's paying the whores?"
THE CANDY: "Nobody beats a Baby Ruth."
X ADVANTAGE: The player

So there you have it; it's so simple when you break things down scientifically. In a squeaker, the advantage goes to Baby Ruth the candy bar. But just remember—both legends can lay claim to the stomachache heard round the world. Me, I'm still fond of the short-lived Super Joe Charboneau bar: It had that curious mix of fudge and a *hint* of smoked salmon. Until next time, I'm Nick Bakay, reminding you the numbers never lie.

JOHN MADDEN VS. ANNA NICOLE SMITH

If size is finally a prerequisite for superstardom, this just might be my year. Case in point, Anna Nicole Smith and John Madden: two tons of fun, and the authors of some big, buxom TV ratings to boot. But in order to truly anoint the XXXL champion, it's time to see how they stack up at the Tale of the Tape…

USED TO BE:
MADDEN: Head coach
ANNA NICOLE: Hot!
ADVANTAGE: Madden

FEAR OF:
MADDEN: Flying
ANNA NICOLE: Salad
ADVANTAGE: Madden

Nick Bakay's Tale of the Tape

BIGGEST WINS:
MADDEN: Super Bowl XI
ANNA NICOLE: Billionaire Lotto
ADVANTAGE: Push

THANKSGIVING TREAT:
MADDEN: The Turducken—a chicken stuffed in a duck stuffed in a turkey
ANNA NICOLE: The Bimboken—cheese, stuffed in a blonde, stuffed in a party dress.
ADVANTAGE: Push! Nobody wins with gluttony.

INSTITUTIONS THEY ARE NOW A PART OF:
MADDEN: *Monday Night Football*
ANNA NICOLE: Sunday Night Geek Show
ADVANTAGE: Madden

SOUNDTRACKS:
MADDEN: "Are You Ready for Some Football?"
ANNA NICOLE: "Devil in a Blue Dress, Purchased from Rochester Big & Tall"
ADVANTAGE: Madden

FAVORITE PART OF SHOWBIZ:
MADDEN: The fans
ANNA NICOLE: The 'dans. You know—Perco, Vico...
ADVANTAGE: Madden

BROUGHT TO OUR ATTENTION:
MADDEN: The V of sweat on a lineman's butt
ANNA NICOLE: The perils of saline
ADVANTAGE: Push

HOW THEY'VE EXPANDED OUR LANGUAGE:
MADDEN: A huge lineman's lower leg is a "kankle"
ANNA NICOLE: An overpriced Mediterranean rental is a "Cana-bana"? Cabanaba? Bullabble labble?
ADVANTAGE: Madden

A SUCKER FOR:
MADDEN: Linemen
ANNA NICOLE: Men—rich men
ADVANTAGE: Push

THEY TAUGHT US HOW:
MADDEN: To transition from the sidelines to the booth
ANNA NICOLE: To make overweight and high a success story
ADVANTAGE: Madden

CUP SIZE:
MADDEN: Suffice it to say his runneth over.
ANNA NICOLE: Industrial?
ADVANTAGE: Anna Nicole

WHEELCHAIR SEX:
MADDEN: Let's hope not
ANNA NICOLE: Not for less than 80 million
ADVANTAGE: Anna Nicole

SHARES A LIKENESS WITH MARILYN MONROE:
MADDEN: No
ANNA NICOLE: Yes
ADVANTAGE: Anna Nicole

SHARES A LIKENESS WITH TONY SIRAGUSA:
MADDEN: No
ANNA NICOLE: Yes
ADVANTAGE: Madden

TOUGH GUYS:
MADDEN: Any member of the All-Madden team
ANNA NICOLE: Her personal assistant, Kimmy
ADVANTAGE: Madden

PREDECESSORS:
MADDEN: Miller and Fouts
ANNA NICOLE: The Osbournes, who now look like aristocracy
ADVANTAGE: Push

ALWAYS TRAVELS WITH:
MADDEN: The Madden Cruiser
ANNA NICOLE: A small, flatulent dog
ADVANTAGE: Madden

CHALLENGES:
MADDEN: Has trouble criticizing fellow coaches
ANNA NICOLE: Has trouble with her consonants
ADVANTAGE: Push

GREATEST ACHIEVEMENT:
MADDEN: The world's first blue-collar star with a six-million-dollar salary
ANNA NICOLE: Made 80 million bucks and still has to work.
ADVANTAGE: Madden

OBVIOUSLY... :
MADDEN: He switched from FOX to ABC
ANNA NICOLE: Switched from protein to carbs
ADVANTAGE: Madden

PARTNER:
MADDEN: Al Michaels
ANNA NICOLE: Whoever says yes...
ADVANTAGE: Michaels, who has had more partners in the last ten years than Pamela Anderson

PREFERRED WRITING IMPLEMENT:
MADDEN: Telestrator
ANNA NICOLE: Nail polish
ADVANTAGE: Madden

WHY AMERICA LOVES THEM:
MADDEN: Vast football knowledge
ANNA NICOLE: Vast tolerance
ADVANTAGE: Anna Nicole—football is great, but messed-up lives make us feel *good* about ourselves!

RELATIONSHIP TO THE WORD "POTATOES":
MADDEN: Couch
ANNA NICOLE: Please pass the...
ADVANTAGE: Push

OFT-HEARD PHRASES:
MADDEN: "Whoomp! Bwap! Blorp!"
ANNA NICOLE: "Mister? How much is them corn dogs?"
ADVANTAGE: Anna Nicole. Hmmm.

LIFE EXPECTANCY:
MADDEN: He's signed through 2007
ANNA NICOLE: Spring
ADVANTAGE: Madden

So there you have it; it's all so simple when you break things down scientifically. In a Vegas buffet landslide, the advantage goes to John Madden. But hang in there, Anna Nicole, you've taught us just how far you can stretch a leopard thong. Until next time, I'm Nick Bakay, reminding you the numbers never lie.

Nick Bakay's Tale of the Tape

MIKE TYSON | MICHAEL JACKSON

Mike Tyson. Gone are the first-round knockouts, and any real shot at the heavyweight belt, and his slap-fests are cancelled and revived more times than Anna Nicole in a room full of pharmaceutical samples. But Tyson still sells tickets because freak shows are hot, baby! Of course, if you saw the Michael Jackson special, you already knew that. But who's the Mac daddy of Freak Mountain? Iron Mike vs. the King of Pop; let's see how they stack up at the Tale of the Tape...

USED TO BE:
MIKE: Baddest man on planet Earth
MICHAEL: Black
ADVANTAGE: Push

CURRENT RANKING:
MIKE: World's highest-paid tin can
MICHAEL: #1 with a bullet...in Superman's Bizarro world
ADVANTAGE: Push

THE BIG QUESTION:
MIKE: Is he off his meds?
MICHAEL: Is his nose going to make it past Tuesday?
ADVANTAGE: Push

POTENTIAL OPPONENTS:
MIKE: Tonya Harding
MICHAEL: Child Services
ADVANTAGE: Mike

DESERVEDLY SCRUTINIZED FOR:
MIKE: Prefight ramblings that make Ozzy Osbourne seem *lucid*...
MICHAEL: The kind of slumber parties a defrocked priest can only dream of...
ADVANTAGE: Mike

REACH:
MIKE: 38", 42" at a beauty pageant
MICHAEL: 36", 40" at a Gymboree
ADVANTAGE: Push

ROLE MODELS:
MIKE: Sonny Liston
MICHAEL: Wayland Flowers' old puppet, Madame
ADVANTAGE: Mike

SCARY MENTORS AND SUPERFREAKS:
MIKE: Don King
MICHAEL: Joe Jackson
ADVANTAGE: Push

QUOTABLE:
MIKE: "That's ludicrous."
MICHAEL: "If all the children in the world were dead, I'd just jump off the balcony!"
I'll just bet you would.
ADVANTAGE: Mike

WE HAVE THEM TO THANK FOR:
MIKE: Buster Douglas
MICHAEL: Four-year-olds grabbing their crotches
ADVANTAGE: Mike

WISH THEY'D NEVER MET:
MIKE: Mitch "Blood" Green
MICHAEL: Martin Bashir, "Documentarian"
ADVANTAGE: Push

UNUSUAL APPROACHES TO CHILD-REARING:
MIKE: Bringing them to boxing press conferences
MICHAEL: Dangling their veiled asses over balconies
ADVANTAGE: Mike

NEVERLAND:
MIKE: Where his next opponent is going to send him
MICHAEL: Home
ADVANTAGE: Michael

CRIES LATE AT NIGHT ABOUT:
MIKE: Don King's bookkeeping
MICHAEL: Having to carry Tito all those years
ADVANTAGE: Mike

DIRTY LITTLE SECRETS:
MIKE: Has developed a taste for Holyfield tartare
MICHAEL: Lowers the height requirement at Neverland rides
ADVANTAGE: Push

EXILED COMRADES:
MIKE: Robin Givens
MICHAEL: Bubbles the Chimp
ADVANTAGE: Push

SECRET FEAR:
MIKE: The book his kids will write
MICHAEL: The book his kids will write
ADVANTAGE: Push

MISINFORMED:
MIKE: Thinks face tattoos are temporary
MICHAEL: Thinks you can buy "art" in a Las Vegas mall
ADVANTAGE: Push

REALLY WANTS FOR CHRISTMAS:
MIKE: His two front teeth
MICHAEL: An Easy-Bake Oven!
ADVANTAGE: Michael

COLLECTIONS:
MIKE: Indictments
MICHAEL: Geranimal bottoms
ADVANTAGE: Push

CORNER MEN:
MIKE: Cut man, trainer, bail bondsman
MICHAEL: Bodyguard, nanny, Miss Butler's fourth-grade class
ADVANTAGE: Mike

So there you have it; it's all so simple when you break things down scientifically. In a Moonwalk with a rabbit punch, the advantage...barely—goes to Mike Tyson, but at the end of the day, these guys will be lucky to get an offer to join the cast of *I'm a Celebrity, Get Me Out of Here!* Until next time, I'm Nick Bakay, reminding you the numbers never lie.

TIGER WOODS
JAMES BOND

It's getting hard to find people who can match up against Tiger Woods. He's suave. He thrives on pressure. He always gets the job done. Men want to be him; women want to...well, you know. Put it all together and only one name offers a suitable challenge: Bond...James Bond. Let's see how they stack up at the Tale of the Tape...

WEAPONS OF CHOICE:
TIGER: Nike
BOND: Walther PPK
X ADVANTAGE: Bond, unless you attended a Jack Nicholson "Pitching Wedge" clinic

ASSOCIATIONS:
TIGER: The PGA
BOND: Her Majesty's Secret Service
X ADVANTAGE: Bond

UNIFORM:
TIGER: A green Masters jacket from the Lawrence Welk collection
BOND: A semiautomatic tux
X ADVANTAGE: Bond

STRANGEST ENDORSEMENT:
TIGER: Buick
BOND: Uh, women?
X ADVANTAGE: Bond

FORMER TEAMMATES:
TIGER: Fluff
BOND: Miss Moneypenny
- - ADVANTAGE: Push

OCCUPATIONAL HAZARDS:
TIGER: John Daly might puke on him
BOND: Oddjob might decapitate him
- - ADVANTAGE: Push

PROVOCATIVE COMPETITOR NAMES:
TIGER: Dicky Pride, Frank Lickliter II, Pierre Fulke, Steve Flesch, Briny Baird
BOND: Octopussy
X ADVANTAGE: Tiger, on sheer volume alone

BIG-BREASTED ENEMIES:
TIGER: Colin Montgomerie
BOND: Pick 'em.
X ADVANTAGE: Bond

NAMES THAT ARE EUPHEMISMS FOR FELINES:
TIGER: Tiger
BOND: Pussy Galore
X ADVANTAGE: Bond

ALSO-RANS:
TIGER: Phil Mickelson, David Duval, Ernie Els
BOND: The Saint, Our Man Flynt, Matt Helm
- - ADVANTAGE: Push

ONE-OF-A-KIND SKILLS:
TIGER: Can tee off with a broom handle and still hit the green.
BOND: Can conceal a chain saw under a wet suit.
X ADVANTAGE: Tiger

RECORDS:
TIGER: An unnatural Grand Slam
BOND: Hit more homers in one season than anyone...Oops, that's Bonds.
X ADVANTAGE: Tiger

BEVERAGE OF CHOICE AT THE 19TH HOLE:
TIGER: SunnyD
BOND: Martini
X ADVANTAGE: Bond, shaken not stirred

EARLY SIGNS OF GREATNESS:
TIGER: Won his first U.S. amateur championship at age 15.
BOND: Bedded his first-grade teacher and got her to give him the answers to the pop quiz.
X ADVANTAGE: Bond

THINGS HAVEN'T BEEN THE SAME SINCE:
TIGER: He joined the tour
BOND: The Cold War ended
- - ADVANTAGE: Push

WANNABES:
TIGER: The Williams sisters
BOND: Roger Moore, Timothy Dalton, Pierce Brosnan, Henry Kissinger
- - ADVANTAGE: Push

MISSION:
TIGER: Rescue the impossibly good-looking Swedish nanny.
BOND: Rescue the impossibly good-looking Swedish double agent.
X ADVANTAGE: Bond

TELEVISION EVENTS:
TIGER: Prime-time one-on-one showdown
BOND: Annual cable movie marathon
X ADVANTAGE: Tiger

SETTING GOALS:
TIGER: How many holes can I eagle?
BOND: How many holes can I conquer?
X ADVANTAGE: Bond

FAVORITE MOVIE:
TIGER: *Caddyshack*
BOND: *Caddyshack!!!*
- - ADVANTAGE: Push. Somewhere, Governor Ventura beams with pride.

So there you have it. In a miraculous escape from an impossible predicament, the advantage goes to James Bond. But hang in there, Tiger, nobody ever gave Bond a free Buick. Until next time, I'm Nick Bakay, reminding you the numbers never lie...

TIGER WOODS
DEEP BLUE

Tiger Woods is so dominant, you get the feeling other tour pros are petitioning to get the minimum age for the senior tour lowered to thirty. So what's our next stop in the never-ending search to find a challenger? How about the monster computer that drove Garry Kasparov to the professional checkers tour? Tiger Woods, Deep Blue, let's see how they stack up at the Tale of the Tape.

REAL NAMES:
DEEP BLUE: A 32-node RS 6000 SP High Performance IBM
TIGER: Eldrick
– – ADVANTAGE: That's a push.

WEIGHT:
TIGER: 170 lbs.
DEEP BLUE: 1.4 tons
X ADVANTAGE: Deep Blue, who might want to try a salad

GOOD LUCK CHARMS:
TIGER: That cute little tiger puppet on his driver
DEEP BLUE: Bumper sticker that says "If the mainframe's a-rockin' don't come a-knockin.'"
X ADVANTAGE: Deep Blue

ENDORSEMENTS:
TIGER: Nike
DEEP BLUE: Napster
X ADVANTAGE: Tiger

AVERAGE DRIVE OFF THE TEE:
TIGER: 310 yards
DEEP BLUE: Four inches. With such a short reach and no knees, he tends to top the ball.
X ADVANTAGE: Tiger

QUOTE FROM BOOK WITH DAD:
TIGER: "Love is a given, respect is earned."
DEEP BLUE: "I always said this kid could kick ass, ain't that right, Delores?"
X ADVANTAGE: Tiger

SNACK FOOD:
TIGER: Chips
DEEP BLUE: Chips!
X ADVANTAGE: Deep Blue! In a shocker!

CAN AFFORD TO BUY A BASEBALL TEAM?:
TIGER: Yes
DEEP BLUE: Too smart to buy a baseball team
X ADVANTAGE: Deep Blue

WHAT THE FUTURE HOLDS:
TIGER: The all-time record for Major titles
DEEP BLUE: Five years says this computer won't be fast enough to run Tetris
X ADVANTAGE: Tiger

FAVORITE WAY TO UNWIND:
TIGER: Video games
DEEP BLUE: Books on tape in which robots have sex with humans
X ADVANTAGE: Deep Blue, and anyone with the gift of imagination

GETS DOWN ON HIMSELF:
TIGER: When he misses those short putts.
DEEP BLUE: When he calculates how many years until the earth collides with the sun, then surrenders to negative thinking.
ADVANTAGE: Push

WEAKNESS:
TIGER: Muscles his short game.
DEEP BLUE: Takes three days to boot up.
ADVANTAGE: Tiger

HAS BEEN LINKED TO:
TIGER: Oldsmobile
DEEP BLUE: That saucy replicant from *Babylon 5*
ADVANTAGE: Deep Blue

HOW TO MESS WITH HIS HEAD:
TIGER: Talk loudly during his putt
DEEP BLUE: Make him share a power outlet with a toaster
ADVANTAGE: Push

EARLY SIGNS OF GREATNESS:
TIGER: Consistently birdied a par five hole at age five.
DEEP BLUE: At five months, explained theory of relativity and scribbled 32,000 scatological Dilbert cartoons.
ADVANTAGE: Deep Blue

FIRST GAINED NOTORIETY BY:
TIGER: Winning three straight amateurs
DEEP BLUE: Sleeping with Frank Gifford
ADVANTAGE: Tiger

SHOWS EMOTION BY:
TIGER: Pumping a fist and a hearty "Yes!"
DEEP BLUE: Spontaneously rebuilding his desktop
ADVANTAGE: Tiger

GUILTY PLEASURES:
DEEP BLUE: Browsing naughty Internet chat rooms
TIGER: Ditto
ADVANTAGE: Push

NICKNAME CONNOTES:
TIGER: Cuddly, yet dangerous
DEEP BLUE: A quiet storm of infinite sex
ADVANTAGE: Deep Blue

ALMA MATERS:
TIGER: Stanford
DEEP BLUE: A tool bench
ADVANTAGE: Deep Blue. How can you like a school that calls itself "The Cardinal"?

CELEBRATES A BIG WIN BY:
TIGER: Crying and hugging family
DEEP BLUE: An approving nod from the Norton Disc Doctor
ADVANTAGE: Tiger

TROPHIES:
TIGER: The green jacket
DEEP BLUE: Unlimited downloads of Jenna Jameson
ADVANTAGE: Tiger—get a green jacket, and you get the girl.

So there you have it; it's all so simple when you break things down scientifically. In a byte-sized birdie on a play-off hole, the advantage goes to Deep Blue! Let's just hope a bitter Fuzzy Zoeller doesn't make any bad jokes about serving Pentium chips at the Masters dinner. Until next time, I'm Nick Bakay, reminding you the numbers never lie.

TIGER WOODS / THE POPEMOBILE

Country club duffers may bring new depths to the words "I suck at hitting a ball," but the game of golf has finally met its match. Question is—will Tiger Woods ever meet his match? Since it doesn't look like that will happen any time in the near future, let's try the Popemobile—the papal golf cart, the world's most impenetrable vehicle and perhaps the only unstoppable force that can rival Tiger's ability to roll forth under any and all circumstances. Tiger, Popemobile—let's see how they stack up at the Tale of the Tape…

WHAT THEY RUN ON:
TIGER: Balata, titanium, and talent
THE POPEMOBILE: Plexiglas, diesel, and guilt
X   ADVANTAGE: Tiger

NEIGHBORS:
TIGER: Mark O'Meara
THE POPEMOBILE: Is often parked next to the Batmobile
   X   ADVANTAGE: Popemobile

WATER:
TIGER: Drives over it
THE POPEMOBILE: Drives on it!
- -   ADVANTAGE: Push—I can't do either…

HOTDOGGING:
THE POPEMOBILE: Can turn on a dime
TIGER: Can fade a shot around a nuclear silo
X   ADVANTAGE: Tiger

SYMBOLIC OF:
THE POPEMOBILE: How Catholics spend their Sundays
TIGER: How the wealthy Catholics spend their Sundays
- -   ADVANTAGE: Push

NEVER LEAVES HOME WITHOUT:
TIGER: "Li'l Tiger" club sock
THE POPEMOBILE: Inflatable Porta-Confessional
- -   ADVANTAGE: Push

CUSTOMIZED:
TIGER: Woods and irons
THE POPEMOBILE: Retractable sunroof for the tall hat
   X   ADVANTAGE: Popemobile

ENTOURAGE:
TIGER: Coach, caddie, girlfriend
THE POPEMOBILE: Fold-down seating for tagalong bishops
   X   ADVANTAGE: Tiger

WHAT THEY HEAR A LOT:
TIGER: You the man!
THE POPEMOBILE: Hail Mary, full of torque!
   X   ADVANTAGE: Tiger

So there you have it; in a sudden-death play-off, the advantage goes to…Tiger Woods. But hang in there, Popemobile—a little modification, and you could be the world's greatest driving range ball-scooper. Until next time, I'm Nick Bakay, reminding you the numbers never lie.

STEINBRENNER VS. CASTRO

When it comes to dictatorial baseball men, no two names inspire more fear and loathing than George and Fidel. Both have ruled with an iron fist for what seems like forever, both have done their part to ratchet up the arms race, but who's *really* da boss? Castro. Steinbrenner. Let's see how they stack up at the Tale of the Tape.

HOW THEY CAME TO POWER:
CASTRO: Viva la revolution!
STEINBRENNER: Viva my father's money!
ADVANTAGE: Castro

BAY OF PIGS:
CASTRO: A close call
STEINBRENNER: David Wells's locker
ADVANTAGE: Push

FALL GUYS:
CASTRO: Che Guevara
STEINBRENNER: Billy Martin
ADVANTAGE: Steinbrenner. Che got fired only once.

MONEY:
CASTRO: Worth about a penny on the dollar.
STEINBRENNER: Worth about a dollar to every small market penny.
ADVANTAGE: Steinbrenner

WHERE DISSENTERS LAND:
CASTRO: A cold prison cell
STEINBRENNER: A cold Montreal
ADVANTAGE: Push

BIGGEST FREE-AGENT SIGNING:
STEINBRENNER: Reggie
CASTRO: Elian Gonzalez
ADVANTAGE: Steinbrenner

FAVORITE CUBAN PITCHERS:
CASTRO: El Presidente
STEINBRENNER: El Duque
ADVANTAGE: Steinbrenner

SARTORIAL STAPLES:
CASTRO: Olive-drab neckerchief
STEINBRENNER: White turtleneck
ADVANTAGE: Push

PLAYER LUXURIES:
CASTRO: A roof on their corrugated lean-to
STEINBRENNER: $8 million to pinch hit
ADVANTAGE: Steinbrenner

4 A.M. :
CASTRO: When his secret police drop by for coffee
STEINBRENNER: When he speed-dials his manager
ADVANTAGE: Push

REVENUE SHARING:
CASTRO: Not ever
STEINBRENNER: Not lately
ADVANTAGE: Push

ABUSE OF THE PEOPLE:
CASTRO: The No! Borders
STEINBRENNER: The Yes! Network
ADVANTAGE: Steinbrenner

TURNED:
STEINBRENNER: Winfield into a pariah
CASTRO: A little island into a threat against democracy
ADVANTAGE: Push

RIVALS:
STEINBRENNER: Red Sox
CASTRO: Miami
ADVANTAGE: Steinbrenner

FIRST TO EXPLOIT:
STEINBRENNER: The free-agent market
CASTRO: The Cold War
ADVANTAGE: Push

COLLECTS:
STEINBRENNER: World Series rings
CASTRO: Human rights violations
ADVANTAGE: Steinbrenner

STRIPED SHIRTS:
STEINBRENNER: His players
CASTRO: Anyone who believes in freedom of speech
ADVANTAGE: Steinbrenner

UNDESIRABLES THEY BANISHED:
STEINBRENNER: Ed Whitson
CASTRO: Boatloads of inmates
ADVANTAGE: Push

PREFERS HIS ARMS TO BE:
STEINBRENNER: Twenty-game winners
CASTRO: Pointed at us
ADVANTAGE: Steinbrenner

NOT AFRAID TO:
STEINBRENNER: Criticize Derek Jeter
CASTRO: Force his populace to throw him a birthday party
ADVANTAGE: Castro

YOU WILL RECOGNIZE THEIR HOME FIELDS BY THE RAMPANT:
STEINBRENNER: Poverty
CASTRO: Poverty
ADVANTAGE: Push

GAVE A BILLION DOLLARS TO:
STEINBRENNER: Bernie Williams
CASTRO: Himself
ADVANTAGE: Castro

WE HAVE THEM TO THANK FOR:
STEINBRENNER: Never wanting to hear "New York, New York" ever again in our lives
CASTRO: The tourist industry in Puerto Rico
ADVANTAGE: Push

DELUSIONS:
STEINBRENNER: Someone out there must like me.
CASTRO: The swing-and-a-miss utopian dream of communism inspired his citizens to see Olympic host cities as turnstiles.
ADVANTAGE: Push

WHEN IN DOUBT:
STEINBRENNER: Fire the manager.
CASTRO: Execute a writer.
ADVANTAGE: Steinbrenner

So there you have it; it's all so simple when you break things down scientifically. Once again, the big-market team bullies the no-market team, and the advantage goes to George Steinbrenner. But hang in there, Fidel. You've still got that "We don't need no stinkin' elections" thing going for you. Until next time, I'm Nick Bakay, reminding you the numbers never lie.

ELIAN GONZALEZ — JUAN GONZALES

Remember the Gonzalez problem? Will he stay? Will he go? Is the grass always greener? And dammit, what's right? Tiger fans were polarized as their agony stretched across the 162-game canvas of a free-agent world...Oh, did you think I was talking about that little Cuban kid in Miami? Both caused disruptions, and both got out. Juan took less to play in a border town. Elian passed on freedom, and also moved to a heavily gated community. Juan, Elian: Let's see how they stack up at the Tale of the Tape.

WHY WOULD ANYONE WALK AWAY FROM:
JUAN: $140 million
ELIAN: Running water
ADVANTAGE: Push

HEADLINES:
JUAN: "Juan Gone?"
ELIAN: "Waco II, Electric Boogaloo?"
ADVANTAGE: Push

$140 MILLION:
ELIAN: His country's GNP
JUAN: A number he will never see again
ADVANTAGE: Push

FAVORITE GAME SHOWS:
ELIAN: Family Feud
JUAN: Who Wants to Be a Millionaire?
ADVANTAGE: Elian

THE MEN PULLING THE STRINGS:
ELIAN: A bearded Commie dressed like Gomer Pyle
JUAN: Señor Greed
X | ADVANTAGE: Juan. He has leverage.

THE SOURCE OF THE PROBLEM:
ELIAN: Border is too close.
JUAN: Fence is too far.
X | ADVANTAGE: Juan

A QUESTION OF:
ELIAN: Free will
JUAN: Free agency
X | ADVANTAGE: Elian

THIS MAY BE THE LAST TIME:
ELIAN: Sees a dentist
JUAN: Sees nine figures
X | ADVANTAGE: Juan

ONE DAY, MANY YEARS FROM NOW:
ELIAN: What was Dad thinking?
JUAN: What was I thinking?
X | ADVANTAGE: Elian. Blame is better.

WAS LEERY OF:
ELIAN: Janet Reno
JUAN: The dimensions of Commerica Park
X | ADVANTAGE: Juan

PROSPECTS:
ELIAN: Braiding beads into tourists' hair
JUAN: Trying to make ends meet on a meager eight figures
X | ADVANTAGE: Juan

FAILED PERSUASIONS:
ELIAN: "Drop the Chalupa and come out of the closet with your tiny hands up!"
JUAN: "Okay, how about $140 million and a complimentary beverage caddie?"
X | ADVANTAGE: Juan

WHAT AMERICA MEANS TO THEM:
ELIAN: The land of screaming people on my lawn
JUAN: The land of a trillion pesos
X | ADVANTAGE: Juan

NICKNAMES:
ELIAN: What's the Cuban word for "Pawn"?
JUAN: Igor, which I believe is German for "Diva"
X | ADVANTAGE: Elian

WHAT HE REALLY WANTED:
ELIAN: An Ipod
JUAN: To make us resent him
X | ADVANTAGE: Elian

STRENGTHS:
ELIAN: Seaworthiness
JUAN: Driving in runs
X | ADVANTAGE: Elian. My, he's yar.

So there you have it; it's so simple when you break things down scientifically. Despite a sofa jammed against the door, the advantage goes to Juan Gonzalez. But hang in there, Elian, only a big-time free agent gets his playmates flown in on the taxpayers' charter. Until next time, I'm Nick Bakay, reminding you the numbers never lie.

BASEBALL CARDS
IRAQ MOST WANTED CARDS

As soon as the Armed Forces distributed playing cards festooned with the fifty-two most wanted Iraq war criminals, they became collectors' items. But that's old news to anyone who collects baseball cards. It's the American way—to smoke our enemies out of their holes, and to turn a silly memento of childhood into a billion-dollar industry. Trade 'em, collect 'em, but by all means let's see how they stack up at the Tale of the Tape...

TYPICAL COLLECTOR:
BASEBALL: Investors
IRAQ: Special Forces
ADVANTAGE: Baseball cards

X

WE CAN:
BASEBALL: Pronounce their names
IRAQ: Connect their eyebrows
ADVANTAGE: Baseball cards

X

EACH PACK COMES WITH:
BASEBALL: Talc-coated, cement-hard chewing gum
IRAQ: K-rations
ADVANTAGE: Push

- -

VALUABLE BROTHER TEAMS:
BASEBALL: Dom, Vince, and Joe DiMaggio
IRAQ: Uday and Qusay Hussein
ADVANTAGE: Iraq, and $30 million

X

CAN ALSO BE USED FOR:
BASEBALL: A bicycle spoke noisemaker
IRAQ: A quick hand of gin
ADVANTAGE: Iraq cards. How many spokes have turned the value of a Mickey Mantle rookie card into less than a Mallow Cup coupon?

X

MOST VALUABLE:
BASEBALL: Honus Wagner, mint condition
IRAQ: Saddam, dead or alive
ADVANTAGE: Iraq cards

X

NICKNAMES THAT INFLATE VALUE:
BASEBALL: Sal "The Barber" Maglie
IRAQ: "Chemical" Ali
ADVANTAGE: Iraq cards

X

BROUGHT TO YOU BY:
BASEBALL: Tops, Fleer, Donruss
IRAQ: Evil, Arrogance, Greed
ADVANTAGE: Iraq cards

X

CONVENTIONS:
BASEBALL: "Living Legends," Cooperstown
IRAQ: "Shock and Awe," Baghdad
ADVANTAGE: Iraq cards

X

AN INVESTMENT IN:
BASEBALL: Infantilism
IRAQ: Freedom
ADVANTAGE: Iraq cards

X

THE MARKET IS DRIVEN BY:
BASEBALL: Grown men trying to recapture the thrill of being nine years old again.
IRAQ: Grown men maintaining the must-kill dodgeball thrill of nine-year-olds.
ADVANTAGE: Iraq cards

X

VARIABLE RATES:
BASEBALL: Whether player makes it to the Hall of Fame
IRAQ: Whether player is alive, buried under rubble, or a grease stain to be named later
ADVANTAGE: Baseball cards

X

COMBOS:
BASEBALL: Together, a set of Ruth, Aaron, Maguire, and Bonds cards are worth more
IRAQ: Uday, Qusay, Saddam, Ghazi, and Rashid = full house
ADVANTAGE: Baseball cards

SPECULATIVE MARKET:
BASEBALL: Sammy corks bat, value sinks
IRAQ: Does seeing a guy's statue head dragged through the city hurt or help his card's value?
ADVANTAGE: Push

ON BACK OF CARD, "K" STANDS FOR:
BASEBALL: Strikeout
IRAQ: Kaboom!
ADVANTAGE: Baseball cards

CHANCES OF GETTING CARD SIGNED:
BASEBALL: It's fifty bucks for Reggie to sign, $70 to personalize it, $100 to make eye contact
IRAQ: Slim
ADVANTAGE: Baseball cards, in a squeaker

FLIP 'EM:
BASEBALL: A game
IRAQ: A precaution
ADVANTAGE: Baseball cards

AXIS OF EVIL:
BASEBALL: Selig cancelled the World Series
IRAQ: Saddam cancelled human rights
ADVANTAGE: Baseball cards

GREAT PLACES TO FIND PLAYERS FOR AUTOGRAPHS:
BASEBALL: The lobby of the All Star Game hotel
IRAQ: Syria
ADVANTAGE: Baseball cards

PROPER STORAGE:
BASEBALL: Mylar sleeves, acid-free boxes
IRAQ: Kevlar vests, acid-rich mobile labs
ADVANTAGE: Baseball cards

OVERRATED:
BASEBALL: Canseco's rookie card
IRAQ: Seventy black-eyed virgins
ADVANTAGE: Iraq cards

SEE PLAYER HIGHLIGHT ON:
BASEBALL: ESPN
IRAQ: CNN
ADVANTAGE: Baseball cards

JOKERS:
BASEBALL: Bob Uecker
IRAQ: The Information Minister
ADVANTAGE: Baseball cards

BEWARE OF:
BASEBALL: Unscrupulous dealers
IRAQ: Surgically altered look-alikes
ADVANTAGE: Push

So there you have it; it's all so simple when you break things down scientifically. In a soaring tater that clears the fence and rolls all the way down Main Street, the advantage goes to baseball cards, but either way, don't lick the laminate. Until next time, I'm Nick Bakay, reminding you that unlike Baghdad Bob, our numbers never lie.

Fans

OFFICIAL MASCOTS VS. UNOFFICIAL MASCOTS

Americans love their official team mascots like they love their cheeseburgers and diet pills. But what about the unofficial mascots—like the scary guy in the Viking suit who has to buy his own ticket to the game. Do we like them? Official team mascots versus self-appointed mascots—let's see how they stack up at the Tale of the Tape.

DOWNSIDE:
OFFICIAL: Chronic chafing
UNOFFICIAL: Chronic vomiting
ADVANTAGE: ...official?

IN COMMON AMONG PEERS:
OFFICIAL: Clown-school dropout
UNOFFICIAL: A need to scream loud enough to drown out the immutable wailing of his inner pain
ADVANTAGE: Oh, move on to the next one...

IN HIS BATHROOM:
OFFICIAL: Lots of talc
UNOFFICIAL: Turpentine, antidepressants, Victoria's Secret catalog
ADVANTAGE: Unofficial

TO THE TOUCH:
OFFICIAL: Furry
UNOFFICIAL: Greasy
ADVANTAGE: Official

SMELL:
OFFICIAL: A little musty
UNOFFICIAL: Downright tangy
ADVANTAGE: Official

TRAINING:
OFFICIAL: Official Mascot University
UNOFFICIAL: Six years at UC, Pilsner
ADVANTAGE: Unofficial

USUALLY LOOK LIKE:
OFFICIAL: Animals
UNOFFICIAL: Deranged, unemployed superheroes
ADVANTAGE: Push

IN HIS HEART:
OFFICIAL: He's tickling everybody's inner child.
UNOFFICIAL: He's flailing at the precipice of insignificance.
ADVANTAGE: Official

ABILITY TO CHANGE THE OUTCOME OF GAMES WITH HIS WILL:
OFFICIAL: Nooo
UNOFFICIAL: Yes?!?! Oh my God!
ADVANTAGE: Unofficial

So there you have it; on the strength of that last one alone, the advantage goes to the unofficial, self-appointed mascots. Don't get me wrong, I still think these guys need counseling. I mean, I wouldn't want my sister to marry one...again. Until next time I'm Nick Bakay, reminding you the numbers never lie.

Nick Bakay's Tale of the Tape

Nothing divides a partisan stadium of fans like the almighty dollar. And what suggests abundant disposable income more than a luxury box at an NFL stadium? But is a tax bracket or twelve the only difference between the fans in a box and the fans in the bleachers? The hoi. The polloi. Let's see how they stack up at the Tale of the Tape…

IN MOUTH WHEN BORN:
BOX FAN: A silver spoon
BLEACHER FAN: A plastic spork
X ADVANTAGE: Bleacher fans—you can't jab with a spoon.

ANCESTORS ARRIVED:
BOX FAN: With the Pilgrims
BLEACHER FAN: With the smallpox
X ADVANTAGE: Box fans

NICKNAMES:
BOX FAN: Scooter
BLEACHER FAN: Jimbo!
- - ADVANTAGE: Push—there are no winners here.

INNER MONOLOGUES:
BOX FAN: "Will my trust dividends exceed what the FDIC insures?"

X BLEACHER FAN: "*Dis* bench is killin' my freakin' butt."
ADVANTAGE: Box fans

LAST CULTURAL OUTING:
BLEACHER FAN: The foreign film section at Costco
BOX FAN: Wrapped in parachute silk at Christo fundraiser
- - ADVANTAGE: Push

WHY HE GOES TO THE GAME:
BLEACHER FAN: Considers it exercise
BOX FAN: So no one will think he's "flamboyant"
X ADVANTAGE: Bleacher fans

WAITING FOR:
BLEACHER FAN: A foul ball to come his way
BOX FAN: His domineering father to die
- - ADVANTAGE: Push

DIRTY LITTLE SECRETS:
BLEACHER FAN: Stashes girly mags under mattress
BOX FAN: Stashes waitresses in walk-ups
X ADVANTAGE: Box fans

SHOWS APPRECIATION:
BOX FAN: By demure applause
BLEACHER FAN: By not hopping the fence and attacking players
X ADVANTAGE: Bleacher fans

So there you have it; it's all so simple when you break things down scientifically. In a Saturday-at-the-mall-with-the-kids landslide, the advantage goes to the fans in the bleachers. Score one for Joe Sixpack, but don't worry, Lawrence of the luxury box—I smell a market correction a-coming that could let you be a bleacher fan, too. Until next time, I'm Nick Bakay, reminding you the numbers never lie.

SPORTS TALK RADIO SHRINK TALK RADIO

Talk radio is a phenomenon with one tragic weakness—the callers. No matter how entertaining and knowledgeable the host may be, there's no escaping the maudlin, self-serving drone of some putz calling in during bumper-to-bumper traffic or, worse, from the bedroom he rents in his aunt's house. Sports callers know it all, except when to hang up and listen. The only time you'll hear more whining and rambling is if you tune in the lost souls who call radio therapists. Then again, what did you expect from a caller who thinks depression can be eradicated from a pay phone? Phone lines are open, so let's see how they stack up at the Tale of the Tape…

SALUTATIONS:
SPORTS CALLER: "First time caller, long time listener…"
SHRINK CALLER: "Hi. I'm my kid's mom…"
ADVANTAGE: Sports caller

TYPICAL SOUND BITE:
SPORTS CALLER: "Hey! Will someone please tell Devil Ray management we cut the retarded third cousin sketch?!"
SHRINK CALLER: "Thaz wright. We shacked up, and now I got this colicky baby and it's hell on earf."
ADVANTAGE: Sports caller

ADVERTISERS:
SPORTS CALLER: Beer, sexual dysfunction clinics, auto malls
SHRINK CALLER: Air purifiers, body-scan clinics, self-help books
ADVANTAGE: That's a push.

WHY THE HOSTS DO WHAT THEY DO:
SPORTS CALLER: Couldn't get the TV gig
SHRINK CALLER: To give their spouses a break from the constant correcting
ADVANTAGE: Shrink caller

HOLD MUSIC:
SPORTS CALLER: Power rock
SHRINK CALLER: Message rock
ADVANTAGE: Push

YOU KNOW YOUR CALL SUCKS WHEN:

SPORTS CALLER: You get interrupted for a pro bowling update.

SHRINK CALLER: The host plays computer solitaire while listening.

X | ADVANTAGE: Shrink caller

BAD STARTS:

SPORTS CALLER: "Hello? Is it me? Am I on? Hello?"

SHRINK CALLER: "Okay, how do I know I'm really talking to Dr. Laura and not to one of 'them'?"

- - | ADVANTAGE: Push

FEEBLE ATTEMPTS AT INGRATIATION:

SPORTS CALLER: "Remember me? We met at your last simulcast from Trophies? I'm the guy with the doughnut pillow and the Boog Powell bobblehead doll!"

SHRINK CALLER: "I'm illiterate, but I still readed all your books."

- - | ADVANTAGE: Push

THE CALL SCREENER HAS BEEN INSTRUCTED TO:

SPORTS CALLER: Disconnect you with extreme prejudice.

SHRINK CALLER: Keep you on the line long enough for local authorities to trace the call.

X | ADVANTAGE: Shrink caller

NO ONE CARES IF:

SPORTS CALLER: You have an epic take on pro volleyball.

SHRINK CALLER: You have sixteen distinct personalities; all of them annoy us with the same screeching voice.

X | ADVANTAGE: Sports caller

WHAT SEPARATES YOU FROM THE PACK:

SPORTS CALLER: You can substantiate a trade rumor because your wife's cousin's mistress claims she banged the team's batboy.

SHRINK CALLER: You believe you can build a strong case that it's actually good to mix booze and pills.

- - | ADVANTAGE: Push

QUALIFICATIONS TO SHARE THE AIRWAVES:

SPORTS CALLER: "Hey, only the unemployed can watch as much sports as I do!"

SHRINK CALLER: "I've been borderline psychotic for years!"

X | ADVANTAGE: Sports caller

IF YOU'RE REALLY LUCKY, YOU JUST MIGHT:

SPORTS CALLER: Win two tickets to a Clippers game!

SHRINK CALLER: Be institutionalized

- - | ADVANTAGE: Push

PEOPLE HEAR WHAT THEY WANT TO HEAR:

SPORTS CALLER: "I know you said we're up against a break, so let me get right to my thirty-six ways to fix the Mets."

SHRINK CALLER: "You keep saying it isn't okay to sleep with my brother, but what if I told you he's a kind man with a really steady job?"

X | ADVANTAGE: Sports caller

So there you have it; it's all so simple when you break things down scientifically. In a photo finish, the advantage goes to sports callers—*barely*. At least they're not talking about themselves. Until next time, I'm Nick Bakay, reminding you the numbers never lie.

GOING TO THE GAME VS. WATCHING IT AT HOME

GOING | WATCHING

If you've delved this far into the book, one thing is pretty clear: You spend a significant amount of your time watching sports. The question is, where? The friendly confines of your home via the magic of TV, or up close and personal at a stadium packed with adrenaline and partisans? Both have their pros and cons, let's see how they stack up at the Tale of the Tape...

DISTRACTIONS:

AT THE GAME: The guy sitting next to you is loud, drunk, belligerent...and the game hasn't even started yet.

AT HOME: Fourth quarter, :38 ticks left on the clock, ball on the three-yard line, and your wife comes in sobbing after a phone call with her mother...

ADVANTAGE: Push

FOOD:

AT THE GAME: Everything from brats to sushi

AT HOME: Inventive nouvelle cuisine such as boiled ham and peanut butter on a bagel

ADVANTAGE: Game

DRINK:

AT THE GAME: A nine-dollar thimble o' watery beer.

AT HOME: Everything you need to blow out a liver before halftime

ADVANTAGE: Push. Happiness lies somewhere in the middle.

THE PRICE YOU PAY:

AT THE GAME: Your money goes to a team owner who is also using your tax dollars to renovate his mistress's luxury box.

AT HOME: It's free, provided the game hasn't been blacked out.

ADVANTAGE: Home—and hello, TiVo!

ATTIRE:

AT THE GAME: Layers and face paint

AT HOME: Hello *Gamederpants*! Also known as the "lucky" underpants you haven't changed since your team started its play-off run.

ADVANTAGE: Game

TAILGATE:

AT THE GAME: A great reason to start drinking on Thursday for a Sunday kickoff

AT HOME: Your wife's bitter nickname for that affair you had

ADVANTAGE: Game

(AND SPEAKING OF TAILGATES, SEE OUR SPECIAL TAILGATE ETIQUETTE PRIMER ON PAGE 39.)

SURCHARGES

AT THE GAME: A massive personal seat license fee for the right to be gouged on the actual tickets.

AT HOME: Your local cable operator makes you buy the Oxygen Network so you can get the game.

ADVANTAGE: Push

TRANSPORTATION:

AT THE GAME: 1 Camry, 8 men, a festival of odors

AT HOME: A Razor scooter to the bathroom

ADVANTAGE: Home

HALFTIME:
AT THE GAME: Anxiously waiting in line for a urinal trough as nachos and beer brew "the perfect storm"
AT HOME: A timely opportunity to spend some quality time with your kids for a solid fifteen minutes
X ADVANTAGE: Home. Remember, it's quality, not quantity.

TRAFFIC JAMS:
AT THE GAME: Coming and going
AT HOME: What happens in your colon when you eat that much cheese
– – ADVANTAGE: Push, hard

YOU MIGHT CATCH:
AT THE GAME: A foul ball!
AT HOME: The Coors Light twins!
X ADVANTAGE: Home

ACTION:
AT THE GAME: You can bet on how many times a guy yacks.
AT HOME: You can log on to the Internet and place some desperation second-half score bets.
X ADVANTAGE: Game, unless the yacker's right behind you.

DEFYING THE ELEMENTS:
AT THE GAME: Shirtless in -12-degree wind chill.
AT HOME: Sans pants, regardless of the broken space heater
– – ADVANTAGE: Push—nobody wants to see you either way.

BLOWING OFF WORK:
AT THE GAME: It's merely coincidence that all your sick days fall during the play-offs.
AT HOME: The festering kitchen trash you've ignored brings back memories of Mom's house.
X ADVANTAGE: Game

HARSH REALITIES:
AT THE GAME: So we can't afford animal protein—it's just for this week.
AT HOME: Can you really clear four consecutive hours uninterrupted by the three F's: Family, Faults, and Fones?
X ADVANTAGE: Game

CHEERLEADERS:
AT THE GAME: Scantily clad on a warm day
AT HOME: Well, your dog has eight perky boobies.
X ADVANTAGE: Game

WHAT YOU CAN SEE ONLY IF YOU'RE THERE:
AT THE GAME: A stadium full of like-minded soccer-mockers
AT HOME: A computer-generated visible first-down marker
X ADVANTAGE: Home—why do I looove that yellow line so?

POSSIBLE SIDE EFFECTS:
AT THE GAME: Wind burn
AT HOME: Barcalounger sweat
– – ADVANTAGE: Push

AFTER A BIG PLAY:
AT THE GAME: You all rise in communal celebration.
AT HOME: No one has to see your very special celebration dance.
X ADVANTAGE: Game

CRAZY GET-UPS:

AT THE GAME: Face paint, cheese head, barrel

AT HOME: Bathrobe so very stank, old KISS T-shirt, your wife's new strappy heels

ADVANTAGE: Push. Remember when men wore suits and fedoras to the game?

ANALYSIS:

AT THE GAME: Annoying play-by-play from the eleven-year-old sitting behind you.

AT HOME: Telestrators, score update crawls, live cutaways to other games

ADVANTAGE: Home

WORST-CASE SCENARIOS:

AT THE GAME: Depression-era Municipal, last row, obstructed view

AT HOME: The tin-foil rabbit ears on the twelve-inch kitchen black and white

ADVANTAGE: Push

POSTPARTUM DEPRESSION:

AT THE GAME: A bumper-to-bumper ride home with nothing but religious talk radio

AT HOME: "He'll never know I missed it. Come on, honey. He's only two! He'll have another birthday next year..."

ADVANTAGE: Push

BEST LEFT UNSAID:

AT THE GAME: "Just once, I'd like to be the quarterback."

AT HOME: "I wonder what my wife and her sister would look like in short skirts and pompoms."

ADVANTAGE: Push

So there you have it; it's all so simple when you break things down scientifically. In a photo finish too close to call, the advantage goes to...going to the game! Sorry, all you homeboys, but there's no glory in training your dog to roll you every hour so you don't get bedsores. But just think, someday in the future we'll be able to watch the game on our cell phones! Wait, that actually wouldn't be so hot. Until next time, I'm Nick Bakay, reminding you the numbers never lie.

TAILGATE DO'S & DON'TS

DO: Designate a driver.

DON'T: Designate the guy who just lit his breath on fire.

DO: Arrive early for prime parking spaces.

DON'T: Swag visiting team banner across the El Camino.

DO: Dress in layers.

DON'T: Wear your "good" flannel shirt. It might get yacked on.

DO: Bring a quart of beer for your neighbor. Maybe he'll reward you with a juicy link of critter sausage.

DON'T: Breathe on the cop when you ask him to help you locate your Firebird.

DO: Establish routes to the latrines before you imbibe.

DON'T: Forget: A city street is not a latrine.

DO: Carry breath mints.

DON'T: Suck on urinal cakes.

DO: Introduce yourself to the ladies.

DON'T: Forget, even inebriated women like flowers the next day.

DO: Have a yearly tetanus shot.

DON'T: Think that means it's okay to lick the mezzanine rail.

DO: Consider wearing a motion sickness patch.

DON'T: Forget, if throwing up is a must, a malted coats the throat and protects it from reflux, and *please* remove all bridge work.

DO: Expose children to the joys of tailgating.

DON'T: Blame them when they fail fourth grade.

DO: Wear bug spray.

DON'T: Be fooled—even in winter, all that public urination attracts flies.

DO: Respect nature.

DON'T: Mistake flies for flying raisins.

BODY PAINTING DO'S & DON'TS

Let's say you're at a point in your life where just going to the game isn't doing it for you anymore. A voice deep inside you keeps saying, "It's time to become a more intense version of *me*." Sound familiar? Then here are a few do's and don'ts for that rare breed who have answered the call to body paint...

DO: Apply paint liberally. You don't want to sweat it all off in the first quarter.

DON'T: Share body brushes.

DO: Use a drop cloth on your swimsuit area at all times. You'd be surprised at the number of bacteria that can "climb."

DON'T: Use white paint after Labor Day.

DO: Look for part-time work in a KISS tribute band.

DON'T: Be surprised if you frighten small children.

DO: Give your character a catchy name, like Captain Dungbeetle, or Kevin.

DON'T: Use clashing colors. You may be wearing them for a long time.

DO: Keep a lot of LAVA soap handy, it's got pumice!

DON'T: Tell your boss that on Sundays YOU have the ultimate power to move thousands of people and one NFL franchise, as in, *I've got the power! I made him fumble!*

DO: Consider a torso shave.

DON'T: Paint over open wounds.

DO: Use a moisturizer under the paint.

DON'T: Expect to "get with" your lady.

PUBLIC GOLF COURSE
PRIVATE GOLF COURSE

Golf—the only game that honestly believes it shouldn't have to hear it from the crowd. When the U.S. Open hit the public course at Bethpage, however, there was more heckling than amateur night at Jumbo's Clown Room. I guess that's the price you pay for getting millions to slap endorsement logos on your bag. Needless to say, the Open has retreated back to the precious, *please whisper* etiquette of the private country clubs, but is privilege and seclusion all it's cracked up to be? Private golf course, public golf course, and what it all means to the average hacker in the gallery, let's see how they stack up at the Tale of the Tape…

PHILOSOPHIES:

PRIVATE COURSE: The etiquette golfers show one another distinguishes golf from all other sports.

PUBLIC COURSE: When you've got twenty bucks riding on the sixth hole, you will break wind at the top of your opponent's backswing.

X | ADVANTAGE: Private course

HEAD TEACHING PRO:

PRIVATE COURSE: Bentley Van Snootington III

PUBLIC COURSE: "Shanks" Dupree

X | ADVANTAGE: Public course—Shanks can fix your follow-through and he knows the best strip clubs near the airport.

IF SERGIO TAKES TOO LONG:

PRIVATE COURSE: Fellow pros politely stand behind him and "go to school" on his putt.

PUBLIC COURSE: The gallery motivates him with a expletive-laced "Hit the ball!"

X | ADVANTAGE: Public course. Nobody wins with a seventeen-hour round.

GALLERY WARDROBE:

PRIVATE COURSE: Tommy Bahama, Cole Haan, Cohiba

PUBLIC COURSE: Wifebeaters, cargo shorts, cardboard "beer in a box" with plastic straw.

X | ADVANTAGE: Public course, and tattoo artists everywhere

HOW THE GALLERY DISRUPTS A CRUCIAL PUTT:

PRIVATE COURSE: An ill-timed cell phone call from someone's broker

PUBLIC COURSE: Seven thousand people, all yelling "Noonan"

- - | ADVANTAGE: Push

KEEPING OLD TRADITIONS ALIVE:

PRIVATE COURSE: Still doesn't give memberships to "those people."

PUBLIC COURSE: At Bethpage, the crowd actually did the wave.

- - | ADVANTAGE: Push—no winners here

HIGH-RISK BEHAVIOR:

PRIVATE COURSE: Asking Mike Ditka if that last putt got caught in his purse string

PUBLIC COURSE: Your fourth is Johnny Knoxville

- - | ADVANTAGE: Push

NICKNAMES FOR TOUGH HOLES:

PRIVATE COURSE: "Amen Corner"

PUBLIC COURSE: "Mulliganville"

- - | ADVANTAGE: Push. Either way you'll never break 100, although Mulliganville does offer a stunning view of the freeway.

WHAT YOU MAY STUMBLE ACROSS IN THE ROUGH:

PRIVATE COURSE: A lost balata

PUBLIC COURSE: A lost body

X | ADVANTAGE: Private course. You can't play through a coroner's van.

WHAT HOSTING A GRAND SLAM EVENT MEANS TO THEM:

PRIVATE COURSE: An excuse to raise the membership fee

PUBLIC COURSE: An excuse to use taxpayer money to re-sod the greens

- - | ADVANTAGE: Push

PLAY-BY-PLAY:

PRIVATE COURSE (WHISPERED): "Tiger... fifteen feet out...yes."

PUBLIC COURSE: "This guy's circling his shot like a dog looking for a dump target!"

X | ADVANTAGE: Private course

"MINDING THE STICK":

PRIVATE COURSE: Proper etiquette when a fellow player is off the green

PUBLIC COURSE: A line you use to hit on the beer cart girl

ADVANTAGE: Push

GREENS FEES:

PRIVATE COURSE: $300 a round

PUBLIC COURSE: Toss your clubs over the fence and make it a fivesome

ADVANTAGE: Public course

WHEN PLAYERS HAVE THE HONOR:

PRIVATE COURSE: They tee off first.

PUBLIC COURSE: They're expected to pay for the hookers in the event tent.

ADVANTAGE: Let's move on...

MARK YOUR BALL WITH:

PRIVATE COURSE: A gold coin with your family crest

PUBLIC COURSE: Let your dog do it.

ADVANTAGE: Private course

TREAT THE GREEN AS YOU WOULD... :

PRIVATE COURSE: A library

PUBLIC COURSE: A former flame back for a quickie

ADVANTAGE: Private course

IF YOU HAVE PROPERLY RAKED THE BUNKER:

PRIVATE COURSE: There will be no trace of your presence after you have left.

PUBLIC COURSE: No one will know that's where you buried an empty forty-ouncer and a bag of Funions.

ADVANTAGE: Push

THINGS YOU MAY HAVE TO PICK OUT OF YOUR PUTT PATH:

PRIVATE COURSE: Leaves, twigs, grass clippings

PUBLIC COURSE: Medical waste, moldy Winston boxes, Coney Island whitefish

ADVANTAGE: Private course

So there you have it; it's all so simple when you break things down scientifically. In a huge win for democracy, the advantage goes to public golf courses, even if they made the pros intentionally hit into bunkers just to get away from the name-calling. Until next time, I'm Nick Bakay, reminding you the numbers never lie.

COLLEGE FOOTBALL FANS

PRO FOOTBALL FANS

Growing up in an NFL town, there was always a part of me that scoffed at the college game. You know what I mean; juniors turning pro, no play-offs, *the wishbone*...but maybe I haven't given these highly paid ama-teurs the old college try. In a world that includes the Arizona Cardinals, which football fan truly has it better? College fans, pro fans, let's see how they stack up at the Tale of the Tape...

RELOCATION:
COLLEGE FANS: When hell freezes over
PRO FANS: When your owner falls in love with a Raleigh-based stewardess
X   ADVANTAGE: College fans

VIGORISH:
COLLEGE FANS: Thousands of dollars in illegal booster bucks
PRO FANS: Thousands of dollars in PSL rights to watch *the Bengals*?
X   ADVANTAGE: College fans

MASCOTS:
COLLEGE: Drama majors
PRO: Unemployed carnies
X   ADVANTAGE: Pro fans

COOL NAMES:
COLLEGE FANS: Cornhuskers
PRO FANS: Packers
– –   ADVANTAGE: Push—both sound like movies currently playing at the Tomkat theater.

PERMANENT FACIAL TATTOOS:
COLLEGE FANS: Little paw prints
PRO FANS: Baltimore Colts...Oops!
ADVANTAGE: College fans

BEST WAY TO MEET YOUR HEROES:
COLLEGE FANS: Share a class with a player, provided you care to repeat fourth-grade arithmetic.
PRO FANS: Encourage your wife to work at a strip club.
ADVANTAGE: Pro fans

DRUG OF CHOICE:
COLLEGE FANS: Grain alcohol
PRO FANS: Prescription-strength Zantac
ADVANTAGE: College fans

CHEERLEADERS:
PRO: Worldly women in spandex
COLLEGE: Fresh-faced coeds being hoisted by guys named "Skip"
ADVANTAGE: The pros...unless you're Skip

THE WORST THAT COULD HAPPEN:
COLLEGE FANS: The death penalty
PRO FANS: Your best wide receiver just got the death penalty.
ADVANTAGE: Push—no winners here...

TRADITION:
COLLEGE FANS: 100 years of Michigan football
PRO FANS: Ladies and gentlemen, your Oakland, I mean Los Angeles, I mean Oakland, I mean...Raiders!
ADVANTAGE: College fans

WHERE ELSE CAN YOU SEE:
COLLEGE FANS: Players kneel and thank Jesus, which they think is spelled with a "G."
PRO FANS: Al Davis wants to hire Jesus, so he can force him to run the vertical offense.
ADVANTAGE: Pick 'em!

CHAMPIONS ARE CROWNED:
PRO FANS: On the field of battle in the Super Bowl
COLLEGE FANS: By a bunch of sports-writers between press box Rob Roys
ADVANTAGE: College fans. Kids, have you ever tried a Rob Roy?

GREAT RIVALRIES:
COLLEGE FANS: Michigan vs. OSU
PRO FANS: The Lions vs. Winning
ADVANTAGE: College fans

AFTER A BIG WIN:
COLLEGE FANS: Tear down the goalposts
PRO FANS: Randy Moss nudges a meter maid with a Lexus
ADVANTAGE: College fans

WHAT PUMPS THE FANS UP:
COLLEGE FANS: School spirit
PRO FANS: The point spread
ADVANTAGE: College fans

So there you have it; it's so simple when you break things down scientifically. In a homecoming-weekend landslide, the advantage goes to college fans! Now if we just get 'em to open *them* books. Until next time, I'm Nick Bakay, reminding you the numbers never lie.

Football

We all assume that a billionaire NFL magnate has it hands down over an unemployed shut-in living over his parents' garage, but is it really that easy? Real NFL owners, fantasy football owners, let's see how they stack up at the Tale of the Tape.

LEAGUE NAMES:
NFL OWNERS: The National Football League
FANTASY OWNERS: The Justice League of America
[X] ADVANTAGE: Fantasy owners, and freedom!

TYPICAL TEAM NAMES:
NFL OWNERS: The Arizona Cardinals
FANTASY OWNERS: The Testosteroons
[X] ADVANTAGE: Fantasy owners—to those who know them, the Testosteroons are synonymous with winning. At last count, Arizona was a decent CFL team.

OUTBURSTS AT OWNERS' MEETINGS:
NFL OWNERS: "Mr. Davis, you can't move again!"
FANTASY OWNERS: "Okay, who cut one?"
[-] [-] ADVANTAGE: Push—there are no winners here.

SALARY CAP:
NFL OWNERS: $67 million a year
FANTASY OWNERS: Whatever's left from the $50 your parents loaned you for that tooth filling
[X] ADVANTAGE: NFL owners

PREREQUISITES
NFL OWNERS: More cash than an entire generation of strippers
FANTASY OWNERS: More free time than Ryan Leaf
[-] [-] ADVANTAGE: Push

HOW THEY MADE THEIR MONEY:
NFL OWNERS: Investments
FANTASY OWNERS: Huh?
[X] ADVANTAGE: NFL owners

TEAM MASCOTS:
NFL OWNERS: An Indian chief riding a horse bareback
FANTASY OWNERS: Bobble-head football doll blessed by Deepak Chopra
[X] ADVANTAGE: Fantasy owners

THE PRICE OF VICTORY:
NFL OWNERS: Rivals raid your free agents
FANTASY OWNERS: Rivals raid your stash of pudding cups
[-] [-] ADVANTAGE: Push

DRAFT LOCATIONS:
NFL OWNERS: Manhattan
FANTASY OWNERS: The house of the owner with the most tolerant wife
[X] ADVANTAGE: NFL owners. Like fantasy guys have wives!

CHEERLEADER TRYOUTS:
NFL OWNERS: Holdin' 'em
FANTASY OWNERS: Holdin' it
[X] ADVANTAGE: NFL owners

YOU ARE RESPONSIBLE FOR:
NFL OWNERS: The hopes and dreams of your city
FANTASY OWNERS: The hopes and dreams of you, and your imaginary friend, Kevin
[X] ADVANTAGE: Fantasy owners. Kevin will never hang you in effigy.

WAR ROOMS:
NFL OWNERS: The grand ballroom of a fancy hotel
FANTASY OWNERS: A folding chair and TV tray near the bathroom
[X] ADVANTAGE: Fantasy owners—did you see that *20/20* with the infrared hotel camera?!

DRAFT DAY NIGHTMARES:

NFL OWNERS: You used your first-round pick on a kid who chooses the ministry.

FANTASY OWNERS: You used your first-round pick on Kordell Stewart.

ADVANTAGE: Push

OWNERS' RETREATS:

NFL OWNERS: Takin' the Lear Jet to Scottsdale

FANTASY OWNERS: Taking your mom's Corolla to Hooters

ADVANTAGE: NFL owners

GAME DAY SEATING:

NFL OWNERS: A luxury box

FANTASY OWNERS: The same Barcalounger you use for "those" movies

ADVANTAGE: Push—you can't put a yardstick on gratification.

WAR CHESTS:

NFL OWNERS: You can always sell a Picasso to sweeten a signing bonus.

FANTASY OWNERS: You can always auction a kidney on the Internet to keep your electricity on.

ADVANTAGE: NFL owners

QUALIFICATIONS:

NFL OWNERS: Lots of green, and the approval of the other owners

FANTASY OWNERS: A ride to the draft

ADVANTAGE: Fantasy owners

THE COMMISSIONER'S OFFICE:

NFL OWNERS: An upscale office in Manhattan

FANTASY OWNERS: A pay phone in a doughnut shop

ADVANTAGE: Push—fines are levied either way.

GAME DAY UNIFORMS:

NFL OWNERS: Vestamente and Ferragamo

FANTASY OWNERS: Underpants and black socks

ADVANTAGE: NFL owners

MEMENTOS OF A WINNING SEASON:

NFL OWNERS: Super Bowl ring

FANTASY OWNERS: Polyurethane beer cozy—hopefully with "Testosteroons" spelled correctly this time!

ADVANTAGE: Push. There are no losers in winning.

CUTTING A PLAYER:

NFL OWNERS: Face-to-face, as his 380 pounds sweat up your leather couch

FANTASY OWNERS: One click of the old mouse

ADVANTAGE: Fantasy owners

HOW MANY TEAMS CAN YOU OWN?:

NFL OWNERS: One

FANTASY OWNERS: As many as your workmen's comp check will allow!

ADVANTAGE: Fantasy owners!

WHAT ADORNS A CHAMPION'S MANTEL:

NFL OWNERS: The Vince Lombardi Trophy

FANTASY OWNERS: A trophy made from empty pudding cups

ADVANTAGE: Push—we need all the heroes we can get!

So there you have it; it's so simple when you break things down scientifically. In a '69 Jets-like upset that may lead to a merger, the advantage goes to fantasy owners! I don't care how rich you are, it's hard to compete with the powers of delusion. But hang in there, all you honest-to-God NFL owners—there's a corporation willing to make you even richer and relieve you of this burden. Until next time, I'm Nick Bakay, reminding you the numbers never lie.

NFL CAMP VS. SUMMER CAMP

Every summer, youngsters from all parts of the country are packed up and sent off to camp—some to frolic near a lake, others to try and make the final roster of their local NFL team. Both destinations guarantee some laughs, some tears, and in most cases a pretty good shot at making it home alive. Summer camp, training camp, let's see how they stack up at the Tale of the Tape.

Nick Bakay's Tale of the Tape

WHAT THEY FEAR AFTER LIGHTS OUT:
CAMPERS: Injun Joe
PLAYERS: The Turk
X | ADVANTAGE: Campers. Everyone knows that Injun Joe's just a legend. Right?...Oh sweet Jesus, what's that behind you?!

FAVORITE CAFETERIA TREAT:
CAMPERS: Ice cream!
PLAYERS: Human growth hormones!
X | ADVANTAGE: Campers

ACCOMMODATIONS:
CAMPERS: A big tent housing three 50-pounders
PLAYERS: A tiny dorm room housing 350-pounders
-- | ADVANTAGE: Push. There are no winners here.

CAMP NAMES:
CAMPERS: Kamp Kissame
PLAYERS: Kamp Konkussion
X | ADVANTAGE: Campers

WHAT WAKES YOU IN THE MORNING:
CAMPERS: Reveille
PLAYERS: The drip of fluids seeping from your impacted spine
X | ADVANTAGE: Campers

MORNING RITUALS:
CAMPERS: Raising the flag
PLAYERS: Raising the sheet
X | ADVANTAGE: Campers

CAMP IS FILLED WITH:
CAMPERS: Kids whose parents crave quality time
PLAYERS: Kids looking to steal your job
-- | ADVANTAGE: Push

GIRLS:
CAMPERS: No
PLAYERS: No, unless you count the kickers. And I do!
X | ADVANTAGE: Campers

YOUR MOM PACKS:
CAMPERS: Candy bars and kisses
PLAYERS: Warnings that you better not come home until you can buy her a house
X | ADVANTAGE: Campers

POISON IVY:
CAMPERS: A rash
PLAYERS: A townie stripper demanding child support
X | ADVANTAGE: Players

BRACELETS:
CAMPERS: Lanyards
PLAYERS: House arrest
X | ADVANTAGE: Campers

LEAST-PREFERRED BUNKMATES:
CAMPERS: Ol' Yellow Mattress
PLAYERS: The rookie who cries a lot
-- | ADVANTAGE: Push. There are no winners here.

ACTIVITIES:
CAMPERS: Canoeing, arts and crafts, hootenanny
PLAYERS: Two-a-days, puking, more two-a-days
X | ADVANTAGE: Campers

FLUIDS:
CAMPERS: Releasin' 'em
PLAYERS: Replacin' 'em
X | ADVANTAGE: Players

IMAGINARY FRIEND:
CAMPERS: Andrew
PLAYERS: Andro
X ADVANTAGE: Campers. Andrew doesn't leave fatty deposits on your liver.

LIGHTS OUT:
CAMPERS: Every night at ten
PLAYERS: The first time you go over the middle near Ray Lewis
X ADVANTAGE: Campers

YOU KNOW YOU'RE IN TROUBLE WHEN:
CAMPERS: It's wedgie season, and you're a husky size 38! (Not that I write from life!!!)
PLAYERS: They issue you jersey #972.
– – ADVANTAGE: Push

LABELS:
CAMPERS: Your mom sewed your name in your clothes upside down.
PLAYERS: You get cut *after* tattooing "Broncos" on your face.
– – ADVANTAGE: Push

TETHERBALL:
CAMPERS: A fun game for two
PLAYERS: Rookie hazing
X ADVANTAGE: Players

WHEN IT'S ALL OVER:
CAMPERS: Your folks pick you up and drive you home.
PLAYERS: Your agent tries to hook you up with an arena team.
X ADVANTAGE: Campers

DREADED MOMENTS:
CAMPERS: "We're putting on a musical"
PLAYERS: "Coach wants to see you, bring your play book."
– – ADVANTAGE: Push!

FATHER FIGURES:
CAMPERS: Your mom's "new" uncle
PLAYERS: The deadbeat dad who resurfaced when he read about your signing bonus
– – ADVANTAGE: Push

BURNING QUESTIONS:
CAMPERS: Will that girl still like me when I get home?
PLAYERS: Will my wife still like me after the vice sweep?
– – ADVANTAGE: Push

DISCOVERIES:
CAMPERS: I've got new hair!
PLAYERS: I think I love our punter!
X ADVANTAGE: Campers

So there you have it; it's so simple when you break things down scientifically. In a panty raid at Hooters, the advantage goes to the players—hey, both rides are humiliating, but at least these guys get paid. Until next time, I'm Nick Bakay, reminding you the numbers never lie.

DALLAS COWBOYS VS. THE GODFATHER

These are strange days in Big D, what with all that glorious Cowboy tradition mired in Bengals-envy. Oh sure, it's hard to stay on top in these days of free agents and salary caps, but we haven't seen the elite fall this far since…well, since *The Godfather: Part III*, when the greatest one-two punch in cinema was chased with a sequel that ranks somewhere below *Dude, Where's My Car?*!

The Bill Parcells era? We'll see. The fact is, dynasties are built to topple, but which of these organizations deserves to be called the most disappointing? The Cowboys, The Godfather: One is quotable, the other potable, let's see how they stack up at the Tale of the Tape…

MASQUERADING AS:
GODFATHER: Olive oil importers
COWBOYS: A viable NFL team
X ADVANTAGE: The Godfather

"I DON'T WANT HIS MOTHER TO SEE HIM LIKE THIS…":
GODFATHER: Sonny's face before the mortician gets to it
COWBOYS: Jerry's face after the cosmetic surgeon gets to it
-- ADVANTAGE: Push

HORRIFYING THINGS THEY LEAVE IN YOUR BED:
GODFATHER: A severed horse head
COWBOYS: A pair of season tickets
X ADVANTAGE: Cowboys

BAD COMBOS:
GODFATHER: Fredo and fishing boats
COWBOYS: Michael Irvin and motel rooms
-- ADVANTAGE: Push

NOT-READY-FOR-PRIME-TIME PLAYERS:
GODFATHER: Sofia Coppola
COWBOYS: Every draft pick since '97
-- ADVANTAGE: Push

"HITTING THE MATTRESSES":
GODFATHER: Hiding out while Clemenza makes sauce

COWBOYS: Hiding at "The White House" while your wife makes sauce
X ADVANTAGE: Cowboys

MAKES KIDS CRY:
GODFATHER: Don Corleone with an orange rind in his mouth
COWBOYS: Barry Switzer with a gun in his carry-on luggage
X ADVANTAGE: Cowboys

SIGNING BONUSES:
GODFATHER: "If there's a suitcase with a million dollars in it, then I'll know I have a partner."
COWBOYS: "If there's a suitcase with twenty million dollars in it, then you can have Deion."
-- ADVANTAGE: Push

IN THEIR POCKETS:
GODFATHER: Four Supreme Court judges and Senator Geary
COWBOYS: Fifty-one bus tickets to NFL Europe
X ADVANTAGE: The Godfather

WHAT MEL KIPER JR. WOULD SAY:
GODFATHER: "Franky Five Angels has a mean streak, and his motor never stops running."
COWBOYS: "Quincy Carter, round three? Major reach."
X ADVANTAGE: The Godfather

DALLAS COWBOYS VS. THE GODFATHER

GOALS:
GODFATHER: To take over the referee union's pension plan
COWBOYS: Uh...win a game?
X ADVANTAGE: The Godfather

OOPS!:
GODFATHER: Letting Appolonia start the car
COWBOYS: Letting Jerry run the draft
– – ADVANTAGE: Push

NOT A WARTIME CONSIGLIERE:
GODFATHER: Tom Hagen
COWBOYS: Chan Gailey
X ADVANTAGE: The Godfather

SPEED MERCHANTS:
GODFATHER: Khartoum
COWBOYS: Bob Hayes
X ADVANTAGE: Cowboys

T & A:
GODFATHER: A type more Greek than Italian
COWBOYS: A cheerleader more saline than flesh
– – ADVANTAGE: Push—everyone wins with pulchritude.

BEGOT:
GODFATHER: *The Sopranos*
COWBOYS: The XFL cheerleaders
X ADVANTAGE: Cowboys—hey, I'm a man with needs.

BIG MEN WITH SMALL BRAINS:
GODFATHER: Luca Brazzi
COWBOYS: Leon Lett

– – ADVANTAGE: Push

DREADED CONVERSATIONS:
GODFATHER: "Fredo, I know it was you..."
COWBOYS: "Coach Landry, we're making a change..."
– – ADVANTAGE: Push

NEVER THE SAME AFTER:
GODFATHER: Sonny hit the tollbooth
COWBOYS: Aikman hit the announcers' booth
X ADVANTAGE: Cowboys

TURNING POINTS:
GODFATHER: "Johnny Ola told me about this place..."
COWBOYS: "Jimmy Johnson is no longer the head coach of the Dallas Cowboys..."
X ADVANTAGE: The Godfather

LET HIM DIP HIS BEAK:
GODFATHER: How respect is paid to Don Fanucci
COWBOYS: How Michael Irvin relaxes
X ADVANTAGE: The Godfather

BAD TRADES:
GODFATHER: George Hamilton for Robert Duvall
COWBOYS: No. 1 pick for Joey Galloway
X ADVANTAGE: Cowboys

AN ABORTION:
GODFATHER: Kay's revenge on Michael
COWBOYS: The title of their team highlight film
– – ADVANTAGE: Push

So there you have it; it's all so simple when you break things down scientifically. In a garroting while an ice pick pins your hand to the bar, the advantage...goes to the Dallas Cowboys! Hey, that's what happens when you reach the top—bitter Bills fans like me take shots at you on your way back down. Until next time, I'm Nick Bakay, reminding you to leave the gun, take the cannoli. Now if you'll excuse me, my boss likes to hear bad news right away...

Musicals and halftime shows—two dinosaurs with an appeal born of a simpler time, when people were so desperate for distraction they gave Red Skelton a career. Personally, I could nap through either, but is it really that simple? A Broadway musical versus a strident marching band, and you—the hapless viewer. Let's see how they stack up at the Tale of the Tape...

MUSICALS

HALFTIME SHOWS

THEMES THEY RARELY TOUCH:

MUSICALS: Life

HALFTIME SHOWS: Death

X | ADVANTAGE: Halftime shows

FEELINGS INSPIRED:

MUSICALS: Now wait a minute! All of a sudden, I'm startin' to feel *sorry* for that darned Phantom!

HALFTIME SHOWS: Imagine if they put that much energy into learning how to read.

- - | ADVANTAGE: Push

CABOOSE OGLING:

MUSICALS: Tight, pert, punished buttocks

HALFTIME SHOWS: The soft, sorry spreads of kids who couldn't make a team

- - | ADVANTAGE: Push—there are no winners with these kinds of agendas.

MUSICALS VS. HALFTIME SHOWS

YOU KNOW IT'S OVER WHEN:
MUSICALS: Somewhere in act one, you find yourself daydreaming about a root canal.

HALFTIME SHOWS: They're chased off the field by the punt team.

X ADVANTAGE: Halftime shows

STAR ENTRANCES:
MUSICALS: The pretty one is carried in on the arms of five guys named Drake.

HALFTIME SHOWS: Someone your parents like is airlifted in via helicopter.

X ADVANTAGE: Halftime shows—and the exciting prospect of technical difficulties.

HOW LONG THEY LAST:
MUSICALS: Long enough to have you stuffing program pages in your ears

HALFTIME SHOWS: Fifteen minutes that will convince you that hell *does* exist

X ADVANTAGE: Halftime shows

THE WORST PART:
MUSICALS: That incessant singing and dancing

HALFTIME SHOWS: Tin vibes amplified loud enough to cause eighty thousand sudden migraines

X ADVANTAGE: Musicals

WHAT THE PERFORMERS SEEM TO BE SAYING:
MUSICALS: "Hey look at me! I didn't get no love when I was little!"

HALFTIME SHOWS: "Please don't look at me, I have built a whole new wing on to the concept of failure."

– – ADVANTAGE: Push—both should be banned quicker than a slitting-the-throat gesture.

WHAT TO WATCH FOR:
MUSICALS: The straight male dancer

HALFTIME SHOWS: The guy who makes the wrong turn

X ADVANTAGE: Halftime shows

SEATING:
MUSICALS: A $100 coffin

HALFTIME SHOWS: A puke-marinated bleacher

X ADVANTAGE: Halftime shows

AUDIENCE PARTICIPATION:
MUSICALS: Try not to laugh during the acting parts.

HALFTIME SHOWS: Hold up your seat cushion to help form a huge can of Coke.

X ADVANTAGE: Musicals

PRICES:
MUSICALS: Enough to guarantee sex from your date

HALFTIME SHOWS: Free, after you've dropped $20 for parking, $75 per seat, and $10,000 for the PSLs.

X ADVANTAGE: Musicals

MISCONCEPTIONS:
MUSICALS: That Americans give a G.D. about the French Revolution

HALFTIME SHOWS: This is better than a fifteen-minute line for the urinal trough.

– – ADVANTAGE: Push

IF YOU'RE REALLY LUCKY, YOU MIGHT SEE:
MUSICALS: Mandy Patinkin get strep throat

HALFTIME SHOWS: A catfight in the clarinet section

X ADVANTAGE: Musicals

SEATS SHOULD COME WITH:

MUSICALS: Cyanide

HALFTIME SHOWS: A peashooter

X ADVANTAGE: Halftime shows

ACOUSTICS:

MUSICALS: Clear enough you can hear every banal lyric

HALFTIME SHOWS: More echo than a Ricola ad

- - ADVANTAGE: Push

WHAT'S AHEAD FOR THESE DEDICATED PARTICIPANTS:

MUSICALS: Opening a tap dance school in Queens

HALFTIME SHOWS: An Internet bidding war for that plastic tuba in your garage

X ADVANTAGE: Halftime shows

WHY WOULD YOU EVER GO?:

MUSICALS: You're a simpleton and your parents raised you with Broadway soundtracks, and yet somehow weren't arrested for child abuse.

HALFTIME SHOWS: Your kid's a simpleton, with a trumpet!

X ADVANTAGE: Musicals

IT'S GOING BADLY WHEN YOU HEAR:

MUSICALS: Programs falling from the hands of the unconscious

HALFTIME SHOWS: Vomit splattering concrete stairs

X ADVANTAGE: Halftime shows—you always feel better after you hurl.

WORD PLAY THAT WOWS THE YOKELS:

MUSICALS: Sondheim finds a word that rhymes with "orange"!

HALFTIME SHOWS: The band spells out "Go Hokies"!

- - ADVANTAGE: Push

TYPICAL DIALOGUE:

MUSICALS: "Hey, everybody—why don't we let Lucy sing her new song!"

HALFTIME SHOWS: "In the 1940s, Americans were swinging to the big band sound!!!"

ADVANTAGE: Someone please kill me

WHEN IN TROUBLE:

MUSICALS: Send a rickshaw for Tommy Tune, but pronto!

HALFTIME SHOWS: Get me *Up with People*, now!

- - ADVANTAGE: Push

So there you have it; in a yawner occasionally punctuated by screams for mercy, the advantage goes to push. Zzzzzzz...Huh? Oh, sorry, must have nodded off. Until next time, I'm Nick Bakay, reminding you the numbers never lie.

While man's challenge against man on the playing field is to score points, his challenge against himself is simple—do it better, faster, higher. Football is a game of strategy. The symbols of that strategy? X's and O's. Every coach would be lost without them, every locker-room blackboard naked, every playbook blank. Mere icons, or so much more? Let's see how they stack up at the Tale of the Tape.

SEEN IN ROMAN NUMERALS:
x: Yes
o: No
ADVANTAGE: X

USED AS A NUMBER *AND* A LETTER:
x: Yes
o: Yes
ADVANTAGE: Push—everyone's a winner.

ALSO CONNOTES "PREVIOUS":
x: Yes (X-spouse)
o: No
ADVANTAGE: X

MAKES NAMES SOUND IRISH:
x: No
o: O'Sullivan, O'Hara—oh yes!
ADVANTAGE: O

USED IN THE WORD "ACCELERATE":
o: No
x: NOOOOOO
ADVANTAGE: Push

USED TO DESIGNATE FILMS WITH "ADULT" CONTENT:
x: Yes
o: No, unless you count the story of O, and I do
ADVANTAGE: Push!

USED TO SPELL ANY PART OF VINCE LOMBARDI'S NAME:
x: No
o: Yes!
ADVANTAGE: O!

So there you have it; in a squeaker, the advantage goes to push! And how fitting, for alone they are merely letters, but together they are synonymous with the gridiron. In this case a tie isn't like kissing your sister, it's like kissing your stepsister, and that's OK! I'm Nick Bakay, reminding you the numbers never lie.

PRESEASON NFL · **RERUNS**

An interesting thing happened on a Monday night a few years back. Thanks to the arthroscopic turf at the Vet, a prime-time, preseason football game was called off and the time slot was filled by the only programming that can rival exhibition football for irrelevance: network reruns. Don't get me wrong, I love my NFL—but it loses its edge when all that bleeding doesn't even dent the standings. I also love my network TV—it puts shoes on my baby's feet, and 92 octane in my luxury car, but God love it, that doesn't mean the stuff is built for multiple viewings, like, say, *The Godfather*. Yet all this moribund viewing be damned, are we about to lift our dimpled hindquarters, risk the heartbreak of movement, and actually see what's going on *outdoors*? I didn't think so. NFL preseason vs. reruns. Both offer sloppy execution and meaningless outcomes, but which is the most doldrums-tastic? Let's see how they stack up at the Tale of the Tape…

MADE YOU CRY:
PRESEASON NFL: A rookie's touching end-zone tribute to his own groin
RERUNS: Whoa, whoa, whoa...Lara Flynn Boyle *out*, Camryn Manheim *in*?!
X ADVANTAGE: Preseason NFL

VIEWING AUDIENCE:
PRESEASON NFL: Overweight single males
RERUNS: Does "viewing audience" include people who just have the TV on?
X ADVANTAGE: Preseason NFL

THEY COME WITH THE TERRITORY:
PRESEASON NFL: Forty-five consecutive incompletions
RERUNS: Wacky neighbors
X ADVANTAGE: Reruns

TIME-OUT FUN:
PRESEASON NFL: A video tour of the turducken coop in the Madden cruiser
RERUNS: "Can you hear me now?"
X ADVANTAGE: Preseason NFL

FILLER:
PRESEASON NFL: Rookies, NFL Europe refugees, Alex Van Pelt
RERUNS: HBO's the making of *The Making Of*
X ADVANTAGE: Reruns

ALTERNATIVE PROGRAMMING:
PRESEASON NFL: TiVo replay of a game from last season
RERUNS: *American Juniors*
X ADVANTAGE: Preseason NFL...and your dignity

YOUR WORST FEARS REALIZED:
PRESEASON NFL: Watching your favorite player blow out a knee while running to the sidelines
RERUNS: Never-before-seen episodes of *Baby Bob*
X ADVANTAGE: Reruns...and pass the absinthe

CLIFF-HANGER:
PRESEASON NFL: Can the Texans master the forward pass?
RERUNS: Will anyone care about *CSI: Scranton*?
X ADVANTAGE: Reruns

THE LAST THING YOU HEAR BEFORE NODDING OFF:

PRESEASON NFL: "And the Falcons are back to punt once again."

RERUNS: "Oh yeah? *You* try to entertain these kids for one day, Raymond."

X ADVANTAGE: Reruns

A FINE OPPORTUNITY TO:

PRESEASON NFL: Surprise your lady with your newfound ability to walk away from the game.

RERUNS: Startle confused onlookers with your uncanny accuracy answering *Millionaire* questions.

X ADVANTAGE: Reruns

COMPLETE UNKNOWNS:

PRESEASON NFL: Anyone playing on the special teams units in the fourth quarter

RERUNS: The supporting cast of that Jim Belushi show

– – ADVANTAGE: Push

JUSTIFICATIONS FOR WATCHING:

PRESEASON NFL: "I'm researching my fantasy football draft."

RERUNS: "Well, I've already tried reading."

X ADVANTAGE: Preseason NFL

YOU'D RATHER BE:

PRESEASON NFL: Watching a game that mattered

RERUNS: Kicked in the stomach

X ADVANTAGE: Preseason NFL

So there you have it; it's all so simple when you break things down scientifically. In a two-part-cancelled-midseason-replacement-season-ender, the advantage goes to...push! Oh m'goodness! I guess it's a toss-up between watching Shane Matthews warming up for the final series or hearing Niles Crane utter yet another delightful quip about wine tasting. Soon, the fall will crackle with real football and season premieres, giving us once again a reason to live. Until next time, I'm Nick Bakay, reminding you the numbers never lie.

Every year, the NFL draft sees dreams realized. For every blue-chip difference maker who gets drafted high enough to buy his mom a Ferrari, there is a draft *fanatic* who brought just as much passion to the Garden, even if he had to drive there in his mother's Vega. These are the men we call Draftniks. They often stay gavel-to-gavel, poring over their stats like some deranged GM-wannabe. Oh sure, all the glory goes to the player, but is it that simple? Draft pick. Draftnik. Let's see how they stack up at the Tale of the Tape...

DRAFTNIKS
DRAFT PICKS

WHAT ARE YOU DOING AFTER THE DRAFT:

DRAFT PICK: "I'm going to Disneyland!"

DRAFTNIK: "I'm going to the Sbarro at Forty-second and Broadway!!"

ADVANTAGE: Push! Wow! I guess I underestimated the magic of a dry plate of ziti.

VICTORY SPEECH:

DRAFT PICK: "I want to thank my coach, my moms..."

DRAFTNIK: "My shop teacher, my sister for lending me her makeup..."

X ADVANTAGE: Draft pick

PAYCHECK:

DRAFT PICK: $8 million over five years

DRAFTNIK: "Hey, I found a dollar in the men's room!"

X ADVANTAGE: Draft pick

IDENTIFYING MARKS:

DRAFT PICK: The classic barbed-wire bicep tat

DRAFTNIK: The classic chest tattoo listing the top five tight end prospects from 1992

X ADVANTAGE: Draftnik—points for originality

STATS:
DRAFT PICK: 4.3 speed in the forty
DRAFTNIK: 4.3 jobs in the last month
ADVANTAGE: Draft pick

RIGHT-HAND MAN:
DRAFT PICK: Drew Rosenhaus
DRAFTNIK: Your imaginary friend, Toby
ADVANTAGE: Draft pick, until Toby gets you a voidable fourth year

HIGHLIGHTS:
DRAFT PICK: A forty-five-second montage of your greatest plays, narrated by Mel Kiper Jr.
DRAFTNIK: A homemade T-shirt commemorating the year you correctly predicted New England would trade down two slots in round six
ADVANTAGE: Push. Hype is hype—we'll see who's for real when we put on the pads.

RARE ACHIEVEMENTS:
DRAFT PICK: You actually graduated!
DRAFTNIK: You're the only one who admits you booed Donovan McNabb.
ADVANTAGE: Push

AND HERE'S THE BAD NEWS... :
DRAFT PICK: Congratulations, you're a Bengal!
DRAFTNIK: Sorry, you're a Bengal fan.
ADVANTAGE: Draftnik—you can always get a dish and spend your Sundays watching a team that actually uses all of its cap space.

Oh, it's all so simple when you break things down scientifically. After further review, the advantage goes to…draftniks? That's crazy. Until next time, I'm Nick Bakay, reminding you the numbers never lie, and I think I better check my math. Pending the recount, all you winners might want to peruse…

DRAFTNIK DO'S AND DON'TS

Like the sparrows to San Juan Capistrano, so do the draftniks return to Madison Square Garden every spring. It can get a little rowdy, but even mosh pits have their own etiquette. In that spirit, I offer up some Draftnik Do's and Don'ts:

DO: Feel free to paint your face.

DON'T: Share brushes with the guy with the pesky, hacking cough.

DO: Arrive early for good seating.

DON'T: Abuse a front-row seat by screaming at the commissioner, "Yo Tags! Wassup! You da man!"

DO: Wear your Oakland Raider meets Gene Simmons pointy armor chest plate.

DON'T: Impale the guy with the bifocals sitting behind you, who is studiously reworking his depth chart of eligible players from Chadron State.

DO: Sit among fellow Steeler fans.

DON'T: Sit among the Raider contingent wearing your "Immaculate Reception" T-shirt.

If you had to pick, which would you rather be—a pro football fan in Cincinnati, or stuck with an HMO that cuts as many corners as Mike Brown? Only the strong need venture forth on this one. Bengals, HMOs, the twin towers of cheapness. Let's see how they stack up at the Tale of the Tape…

SUPERSECRET CORPORATE MOTTOES:
BENGALS: "A complete NFL roster for the price of a utility infielder!"
HMO: "Man, can we turn those beds over!"
ADVANTAGE: Push

WHY SO PROUD?:
BENGALS: "We're millions under the cap, again!"
HMO: Pocketing undertaker kickbacks since 1982!
ADVANTAGE: Push

BOTTOM LINE:
BENGALS: Throw nickels around like hubcaps.
HMO: Diagnosis, schmiagnosis, it's just a cold!
ADVANTAGE: Push

THE PRESCRIPTION:
BENGALS: Rub some dirt on it.
HMO: Throw some dirt on him.
ADVANTAGE: Push

SIGNS OF TROUBLE:
BENGALS: The Whirlpool has algae.
HMO: Recycled needles and crusty morphine
ADVANTAGE: Push

YOU'RE NOT GOING ANYWHERE:
BENGALS: Slap the franchise tag on you.
HMO: Slap a "do not resuscitate" tag on your toe.
ADVANTAGE: Bengals—hey, it's for one year, not eternity.

MORE CORNERS CUT:
BENGALS: The team doctor works for Costco coupons.
HMO: You're covered for a tent and one aspirin.
ADVANTAGE: Push

THEY RARELY… :
BENGALS: Score touchdowns
HMO: Cure you
ADVANTAGE: Bengals

PAINKILLERS:
BENGALS: The off-season
HMO: Going toward the light
ADVANTAGE: Push

CHOW TIME:
BENGALS: Pregame meals at Denny's
HMO: All the water you want!
ADVANTAGE: Push

TRAVEL:
BENGALS: Mini Cooper shuttles you from the hotel to the stadium.
HMO: A teamster with a hand truck hauls you and a crate of rubber gloves to the ER.
ADVANTAGE: Push

PROGNOSIS:
BENGALS: Turned a project like Akili Smith into a decent high school QB, and now it's Carson Palmer's turn.
HMO: Morphed your toenail fungus into gangrene.
ADVANTAGE: Push

So there you have it; it's all so simple when you break things down scientifically. In a defibrillator-come-back special, the advantage goes to the Bengals. But hang in there, all you HMOs—with all the money you've saved, why not grab up the naming rights to the Bengals new crib? I can just see it now—"Good evening, ladies and gentlemen, and welcome to Share a Catheter Stadium!" I feel better already. Until next time, I'm Nick Bakay, reminding you the numbers never lie.

DO-IT-YOURSELF HALL OF FAME SPEECH

Much is made of how the toughest men melt and watch salty tears drip on their Canton blazers until they bleed yellow, but not enough is made of the speeches, which, despite their sincerity, tend to be more formulaic than a Spielberg blockbuster. For any potential inductees who have procrastinated writing a Hall of Fame speech, we humbly offer what we at Team Bakay Inc. call the All-Purpose Hall of Fame Speech Template. Normally we charge enormous consulting fees for this service, but we'll float you this one on good faith. We went with the short form, because brevity is the soul of wit, your memory ain't what it used to be, and studies have shown that weepy interludes are guaranteed to tack an extra ten minutes onto your prepared materials. Just customize wherever indicated, and take that podium for the ride of its life.

YOUR CUSTOMIZED PRO FOOTBALL HALL OF FAME SPEECH

I'd like to thank [1] for presenting me. That was a [2] introduction, and a reminder to us all why they called you [3]. It's an honor to stand beside my fellow inductees. What great men, what [4]! In particular, it means so much to be entering the Hall with [5]—I'll never forget [6]. [7], I was just a [8] fresh out of [9]. Standing at this podium today, I realize I've come a long way from [10]. I see a lot of smiling faces out there. Family, former teammates, and the fans—especially those of you who drove all the way [11]. I've always said [12] fans are the best fans in the world.

(Wait for applause, start to get weepy.)

Come on, [13]. I promised myself I wouldn't [14].

(Long pause to regain composure, control chin quiver.)

No one gets here [15]. The game of football [16]. Thank you for making all of my [17].

(Now walk off like the legend you are.)

1:		2:	
	• my coach		• helluva
	• my minister		• Hail Mary of an
	• my uncle who's never had nothin'		• brutally honest
	• my sister who don't get out much		• long-winded and self-congratulatory
	• my shrink—without these meds, doc...		• surreal and confusing
	• my anger management counselor	**3:**	• the best in the game
	• last year's reigning Miss Universe		• the man who defined the essence of
	• Paris Hilton		squatting low and firing off the line
	• Spalding Gray		• Ol' Puke Breath
			• a supplement-fueled psychopath

4:	• great warriors • magnificent bastards • blood-lusting mercenaries • sweet-ass slabs of man-meat	**10:**	• the cornfields of Nebraska • the South Side of Chicago • the mean streets of Grosse Pointe, Michigan
5:	• (name of older player/contemporary you admired) • (name of opponent you never really liked and made your life hell on the field) • (name of teammate who split your votes, thereby keeping both of you out of the hall for years)	**11:**	• from (your team's hometown) • just to avoid quality time with your families
		12:	• (your team's name)
		13:	• (your first name) • (your jersey number—as in "Old number 99") • jackass • wuss
6:	• that Super Bowl—it's a shame someone had to lose that day • the disturbing things you used to yell at me right before the snap • the way your eyes glazed over when your amphetamines kicked in • the way you snapped my femur • the way you ran to the sidelines to avoid getting hit	**14:**	• cry • snork • blow an emotional snot bubbler • choke on my own sense of unworthiness
		15:	• alone • without painkillers
		16:	• is like life • is why I'm rich
7:	• In 1989 • More summers/battles/wars/years/lawsuits ago than I can remember • Back when I could still put my own pants on in the morning	**17:**	• dreams come true • nightmares become reality • lame restaurants succeed, just because they have a lot of team banners and crap
8:	• young kid • crazy dreamer • rookie with a $10 million signing bonus		
9:	• school • an unaccredited JUCO • the state pen		

Great speeches, like championships, are built in your preparation. Do your homework, write extra large on index cards, and for God's sake bring a hanky.

NFL FOOTBALL / SOCCER

Why is it that some of the more macho cultures like Brazil, Mexico, and Italy play the world's softest game? Soccer is for sissies. England tries to toughen soccer's image by *calling* it football, but everyone knows it's not football. Soccer, "the world's game," versus football, "the man's game." Let's see how they stack up at the Tale of the Tape…

TYPICAL FINAL SCORE:
FOOTBALL: 24–17
SOCCER: None
ADVANTAGE: Football

DO THEIR JERSEYS HAVE NUMBERS?:
FOOTBALL: Yes
SOCCER: Yes, but they're metric
ADVANTAGE: Football

AS A RULE:
SOCCER: Players can't use their hands.
FOOTBALL: Players can't use their brains.
ADVANTAGE: Football—you aren't paid to think out there!

HALFTIME ENTERTAINMENT:
FOOTBALL: Cheerleaders
SOCCER: Gauchos
ADVANTAGE: Soccer?!

STADIUM FOOD:
FOOTBALL: Hot dogs and beer
SOCCER: Goat'n'guava smoothies
ADVANTAGE: Football

STADIUM MUSIC:
SOCCER: "The Macarena"
FOOTBALL: "Rock'n'Roll, pt. 2"
ADVANTAGE: Push, no winners here.

DIET:
FOOTBALL PLAYER: Meat, potatoes, ephedra-laced Lunchables
SOCCER PLAYER: Insects, fruit, and mojitos
ADVANTAGE: Football (Insects? Pass…)

INSTINCTIVE VICTORY CELEBRATION:
SOCCER: A tush-pattin' pileup
FOOTBALL: A dry-humpin' solo in the end zone
ADVANTAGE: Push…and I'm feelin' a tad *queasy.*

AVERAGE BUILD:
FOOTBALL PLAYER: 240 lbs., engorged necks, except for the kicker
SOCCER PLAYER: Like a kicker's
ADVANTAGE: Football

BALL SHAPE:
FOOTBALL: Oblong
SOCCER: Round
ADVANTAGE: Football. As for soccer, you might want to have that looked at.

PRIMARY USE OF HEAD:
SOCCER: To score
FOOTBALL: To impale
ADVANTAGE: Football

So there you have it; it's so simple when you break things down scientifically. In a summer full of two-a-days, the advantage goes to football. Soccer can go off and cry in the corner, like a baby…look at you…You sicken me and every other red-blooded football fan. I'm Nick Bakay, reminding you the numbers never lie.

Kickers. They're like girls. They have poor upper-body strength, they cry easily, and they cost me money! What else can you say as you watch three cover points veering to the shtoink side of the uprights? When it comes to high-profile gigs with small workloads, the only other person who comes close is Santa Claus. Think about it—both watch others do the heavy lifting, then grab all the glory when things go well. I think it's time to see how they stack up at the Tale of the Tape...

KICKERS
SANTA CLAUS

IF YOU'VE BEEN NAUGHTY:
KICKERS: Leave you one point shy of beating the point spread
SANTA: Leaves you a lump of coal
X   ADVANTAGE: Santa—you'll need that coal for heat after you're evicted.

ACTUAL WORKING HOURS, ANNUALLY:
KICKERS: 3.5
SANTA: 24
X   ADVANTAGE: Kickers

TABLE SETTERS:
KICKERS: Eleven real football players
SANTA: 306 p.o.'d elves
X   ADVANTAGE: Kickers

HEIGHT:
KICKERS: 5' 4"
SANTA: Has anybody actually seen him standing up?
X   ADVANTAGE: Santa—no way Kringle don't tower over a specialist.

WEIGHT:
KICKERS: A fawnish 168
SANTA: A gelatinous 380
X ADVANTAGE: Santa, the classic run plugging nose tackle.

ALIASES:
KICKERS: Mr. Blame It on My Bunion
SANTA: A bus and truck Wilford Brimley
ADVANTAGE: Push

SHOES:
KICKERS: A mismatched pair of cleats and dainty Capezios
SANTA: Matching black boots
ADVANTAGE: Santa

YO' MAMMA:
KICKERS: I saw Sebastian Janikowski slipping her a roofy...
SANTA: She said he hung the mistletoe *where*?!
ADVANTAGE: Push—no one wins with childhood trauma.

SIGNS OF GENDER CONFUSION:
KICKERS: Soccer style
SANTA: Support hose
ADVANTAGE: Push

BEARDS:
KICKERS: Only at team functions when a date is required
SANTA: Yes, and it stinks
ADVANTAGE: Push

BIGGEST FEAR:
KICKERS: Huge linemen will tape me to the shower wall...again.
SANTA: Delivering gifts to known chubby-chasers
X ADVANTAGE: Santa—it's always nice to be wanted.

MUTUAL ENVY:
KICKERS: Is that coat lined with sable?!?
SANTA: Those Grammaticas sure would make good elves
ADVANTAGE: Push

I.R.:
KICKERS: Hangnail on big "money" toe
SANTA: Rein burn, soot allergy, and of course, gout
ADVANTAGE: Push. Ya gotta play hurt.

MARTYRS:
KICKERS: Scott Norwood
SANTA: Look, I know it's his friggin' birthday, but who's the man hauling the PlayStation 2s to your mewling little brats? Am I right? Show of hands? Hellooo?
X ADVANTAGE: Kickers

HAILS FROM:
KICKERS: Any nation with eight vowels in its name
SANTA: The North Pole, by way of Stuckeys
ADVANTAGE: Push

MOMENTS THAT WILL LIVE IN IGNOMINY:
KICKERS: Garo Yepremian's "forward" pass
SANTA: The year he put *The Internet for Dummies* under Pete Townshend's tree
ADVANTAGE: Push

OFTEN DOWN WIND OF:
KICKERS: "Squirts," the long-snapper
SANTA: "Fajita," one of the less-publicized reindeer
ADVANTAGE: Push

HANGOUTS:
KICKERS: Piano bars
SANTA: The North Pole Hooters
X ADVANTAGE: Santa

LIFE EXPECTANCY:
KICKERS: Till his teammates toss him out of the plane over Cleveland after blowing three chip shots in O.T.
SANTA: Forever, or until the jihad brings down our craven icons
- - ADVANTAGE: Push

DREADS:
KICKERS: No time left, 2-point game, into the wind
SANTA: 2 A.M. over Kabul
X ADVANTAGE: Kickers

KEEPS WARM WITH:
KICKERS: One of those little jersey muffs
SANTA: Blitzen?! Oh dear...
X ADVANTAGE: Kickers

PREGAME MEAL:
KICKERS: Mueslix
SANTA: Something vegan, since his Lipitor ran out
X ADVANTAGE: Kickers

SOFT BALLS:
KICKERS: The kind he likes to kick
SANTA: Since '69
X ADVANTAGE: Kickers

GLAD TO SEE THE END OF:
KICKERS: Any hope he'll make a tackle on kick returns
SANTA: Cabbage Patch Kids
- - ADVANTAGE: Push

THE HOT NEW TOY:
KICKERS: The punter
SANTA: Grand Theft Auto
X ADVANTAGE: Santa

SECRET SHAME:
KICKERS: Sometimes I flop for fifteen yards.
SANTA: Sometimes I skip houses that don't have cable.
- - ADVANTAGE: Push

WHAT THEY WANTED TO BE WHEN THEY GREW UP:
KICKERS: Beckham
SANTA: The Easter Bunny
- - ADVANTAGE: Push

NAUGHTY OR NICE?:
KICKERS: Considers the entire concept too judgmental
SANTA: Favorite role-playing game with Mrs. Claus
X ADVANTAGE: Santa

So there you have it; it's all so simple when you break things down scientifically. In a holly jolly late hit over the middle, the advantage goes...to Santa. But hang in there, you soccer-style minxes, for some reason, you still get a play-off share. Until next time, I'm Nick Bakay, reminding you the numbers never lie...

Tales of
Two Cities

NEW ORLEANS VS. SALT LAKE CITY

NEW ORLEANS   SALT LAKE CITY

In one magical winter, the Olympics were in Salt Lake City, and the Super Bowl was in New Orleans—thus a tale of two cities best described as the Beaver Cleaver and Eddie Haskell of metropolii. Enablement? Repression? Not to say everyone in Utah is a Mormon, or that no one in New Orleans is a teetotaler, but in the immortal words of J. J. Hunsecker, "Are we kids, or what?" In the meantime: The Big Easy versus The Big Teasey—let's see how they stack up at the Tale of the Tape...

LATTER-DAY SAINTS:
SALT LAKE CITY: Joseph Smith
NEW ORLEANS: Aaron Brooks
ADVANTAGE: Push

POLYGAMY:
SLC: An ugly remnant of the past
NO: A savory promise of tomorrow
X ADVANTAGE: Salt Lake City

VOODOO:
SLC: Convincing the IRS that cults are tax-exempt
NO: Sprinkling gris-gris on your enemy's doorstep
X ADVANTAGE: Salt Lake City

OXYMORONS:
SLC: The Utah Jazz
NO: The New Orleans Moderation
ADVANTAGE: Push

FROWNED UPON:
SLC: Caffeine
NO: Sleep
ADVANTAGE: Push

MISSIONARY:
SLC: A two-year commitment
NO: A starting position
ADVANTAGE: Push

Nick Bakay's Tale of the Tape

GARMENTS:
SLC: The last wall of defense between you and your naughty place
NO: What the stripper just threw in your face
ADVANTAGE: New Orleans

POPULAR MISCONCEPTIONS:
SLC: Karl Malone works for the post office.
NO: Dr. John is a cardiologist.
ADVANTAGE: Push, and for the record, Merlin Olsen had nothing to do with the sword in the stone.

ANNOYING MUSICAL DYNASTIES:
SLC: The Osmonds
NO: The Marsalises
ADVANTAGE: Push

THE STREETS ARE PAVED WITH:
SLC: Guilt
NO: Vomit
ADVANTAGE: Push

TYPICAL VISITORS:
SLC: Purists
NO: Tourists
ADVANTAGE: Push

HAPPY HOURS:
SLC: Twelfth of never
NO: 24/7
ADVANTAGE: New Orleans

SUNDAY ACTIVITIES:
SLC: Sitting in a pew
NO: Stewing in your goo
ADVANTAGE: Push

HOW TO SEE A NAKED WOMAN:
SLC: Propose, then wait five years.
NO: Throw her some Mardi Gras beads.
ADVANTAGE: New Orleans

FUNK:
SLC: The Mormon Tabernacle Choir sing Snoop Dogg
NO: The Meters
ADVANTAGE: New Orleans, although the Tabs knock "Gin 'N Juice" out of the park.

HOT SPOTS:
SLC: Abstinence Alley
NO: Bourbon Street
ADVANTAGE: New Orleans

REGRETS:
SLC: The Taliban came up with the burka first.
NO: Tom Benson's sideline parasol dance
ADVANTAGE: Push

WORDS TO LIVE BY:
SLC: Perhaps another piece of pie will take away the tingle in my pants.
NO: Pity the people who don't drink, because when they wake up in the morning, that's as good as they're gonna feel all day.
ADVANTAGE: Push

So there you have it; it's all so simple when you break things down scientifically. In a hedonistic frenzy worthy of *Girls Gone Wild*, the advantage goes…to New Orleans. Biased? You bet, but hang in there, Salt Lake City—I'm sure I'll regret the whole thing when I wake up with a headache tomorrow. Until next time, I'm Nick Bakay, reminding you the numbers never lie.

USA
BRAZIL

I hate soccer. The more I watch it, the more I trace its lineage to Kick the Can. But I've come to love the passion of World Cup Soccer—this isn't Cleveland versus Dallas, it's us against them! Sport is war, and I'm ready to hate anyone in our path. Why? Because they're different! Our beer is cold, theirs is warm; we have a "civilization," they are "wandering nomads," whatever! So here we go, America versus Brazil, let's see how they stack up at the Tale of the Tape.

NUMBER OF WINS IN HEAD-TO-HEAD COMPETITION:
BRAZIL: 5
AMERICA: 0
X ADVANTAGE: Brazil

NUMBER OF WORLD CUP CHAMPIONSHIPS:
BRAZIL: 3
AMERICA: 0
X ADVANTAGE: Brazil

TOP EXPORT:
AMERICA: Everything good that the world wants!
BRAZIL: Some puppets and shiny beads
X ADVANTAGE: USA!

TRADITIONAL CATTLE HERDERS:
AMERICA: Cowboys
BRAZIL: Gauchos
X ADVANTAGE: USA

SUPERSTITIONS:
AMERICA: Break a mirror, seven years of bad luck.
BRAZIL: If you don't leave corn for the Monkey God, he will steal your breath in the night.
ADVANTAGE: USA

ACTION SNACK:
AMERICA: Snickers
BRAZIL: Iguanas
ADVANTAGE: USA. Snickers, it satisfies you!

MOST BELOVED ROCK 'N ROLL ANTHEM:
AMERICA: "Slow Ride," Foghat!
BRAZIL: None, unless you count Duran Duran's "Rio"...and I don't!
ADVANTAGE: USA

KIDS DREAM OF:
AMERICA: Growing up to be doctors and lawyers
BRAZIL: Cleaning doctors' and lawyers' houses
ADVANTAGE: Push...Huh?!?

Hey, I know I'm in your face, Brazil, but this is my country, baby! Besides, in soccer I get one goal every ninety minutes—score more and I don't have to find such nasty ways to stay interested!

DEEPEST SECRET:
AMERICA: Don't tell anyone, but we're already sick of Tony Meola.
BRAZIL: Don't tell anyone, but we still think fire is a person.
ADVANTAGE: USA

AFTER THE WORLD CUP, SPORTS FANS TURN THEIR ATTENTION TO:
AMERICA: The World Series
BRAZIL: The Frog Races
ADVANTAGE: USA

PLAYERS START EACH DAY:
AMERICA: Watching the *SportsCenter* rerun
BRAZIL: Checking their shoes for scorpions
ADVANTAGE: USA

WHAT HAPPENS WHEN THE REF BLOWS A CALL:
AMERICA: A playful chant along the lines of "The ref forgot his lunch, eat it ref, eat it!"
BRAZIL: The womenfolk carry his head on a stick through the marketplace.
ADVANTAGE: Brazil!

REACTION TO A BLOWN CORNER KICK:
AMERICA: "I didn't hit it well."
BRAZIL: "Aaaaiieee! The ball has elves in it!"
ADVANTAGE: USA

So there you have it; it's so simple when you break things down scientifically. In a stunning upset the advantage goes to Us, even though They usually beat us! Wrap this one in Old Glory, bake an apple pie, and shag a healthy whiff of freedom, baby. Why? What other country would allow me to crack wise like this? Just another reminder that in America, the numbers never lie. Well, almost never...

BRISTOL
NEW YORK

Why is ESPN headquartered in Bristol, Connecticut? Was Podunk taken? It's easy to control a local political climate that resembles Mayberry? Because Berman already lived there? Or did the brain trust at ESPN see an advantage in setting up camp miles away from the twinkle of an urban media center like, say…New York City? The Big Apple versus Satellite Dish Row, let's see how they stack up at the Tale of the Tape.

ON A CLEAR DAY, YOU CAN SEE:
NEW YORK: Forever
BRISTOL: All the way to Larry Biehl's old house!
ADVANTAGE: New York

FAMOUS RESTAURANTS:
NEW YORK: Le Cirque
BRISTOL: Friendly's
ADVANTAGE: Bristol. I don't recall Le Cirque offering a 10 percent discount to ESPN employees, or a strawberry Fribble!

MANY LOCALS:
NEW YORK: Can't speak English
BRISTOL: Can't speak without a producer in their ear
ADVANTAGE: Push

TIMELESS CATHEDRALS:
NEW YORK: Yankee Stadium
BRISTOL: Once again, Friendly's!
ADVANTAGE: Bristol

COLLEGES:
NEW YORK: Columbia
BRISTOL: Legendary Briarwood College
ADVANTAGE: New York

ARCHITECTURAL CONUNDRUMS:
NEW YORK: The triangular Flatiron Building
BRISTOL: The Otis Elevator test shaft
ADVANTAGE: Bristol—tell me this death drop wasn't meant to host an X Games event! And New York without elevators is called Omaha, Nebraska!

AMUSEMENT PARKS:
NEW YORK: Coney Island, home of the Cyclone
BRISTOL: Lake Compounce—the oldest amusement park in the nation!
ADVANTAGE: Bristol! If you're a thrill seeker, nothing gets adrenaline fizzing through your veins like the combination of the words "roller coaster" and "world's oldest"!

OH I WISH I WAS:
NEW YORK: An Oscar Meyer wiener
BRISTOL: An intern on *Kiana's Flex Appeal*! Ungowah!
ADVANTAGE: Bristol

LIBRARIES:
NEW YORK: The Public
BRISTOL: That's what they call the bathroom.
ADVANTAGE: Bristol—nobody ever shushes you there.

HOME OF:
BRISTOL: *The World's Strongest Man*
NEW YORK: The world's strongest-smelling man
ADVANTAGE: Push

ANNUAL UNVEILINGS:
NEW YORK: The Christmas tree at Rockefeller Center
BRISTOL: Mel Kiper Jr.!
ADVANTAGE: Bristol—show me one pine tree that can tell me a JUCO transfer's time in the forty!

IS THERE A MUSEUM DEVOTED TO THE HISTORY OF CLOCKS AND WATCHES?:
NEW YORK: No
BRISTOL: Yes!
ADVANTAGE: Bristol, and don't even get me started on the Lock Museum of America—in your face, Guggenheim!

HEALTH CARE:
NEW YORK: Many fine research hospitals
BRISTOL: A knife, some whiskey, and the steady hands of Charlie Steiner
ADVANTAGE: Bristol—Charlie removed my gall bladder and never charged me a dime!

So there you have it; in a street fight, the advantage goes to Bristol! But hang in there, New York—since the ESPN Zone restaurant opened in Times Square, it's getting harder to tell the cities apart. Until next time, I'm Nick Bakay, reminding you the numbers never lie.

Having grown up in a border town called Buffalo, I considered it a great honor to contribute this segment between periods during ESPN's coverage of the 1999 Eastern Conference Finals, and savored the opportunity to even a long-standing score in one of hockey's better regional rivalries.

When Buffalonians and Torontonians meet, we often spend the time deriding each other's hockey teams and the local television programming we shared in our youth. Canadians delight in Eyewitness News's *Irv Weinstein reporting yet another case of arson on the East Side—the lead story in Buffalo for a good twenty years. Americans retaliate with surreal CBC shows like* Tiny Talents, *which invariably featured a seven-year-old accordion player from St. Catherines, or* The Party Game, *which starred obscure Canadian "celebrities" playing charades. At the end of the day, the strangest place to grow up gets a big Push. With apologies to my mom, who was born and raised in Edmonton, Alberta, away we go...*

Buffalo and Toronto—a gritty punch line in the northern corner of a superpower vs. the fanciest city in a country whose entire population could fit in Ken Hitchcock's old pants. I should admit I grew up five minutes from the Peace Bridge in Buffalo, but my mom's Canadian, so I'm going to *try* to be very objective here. Sabres versus Maple Leafs: The only Canadian team in the play-offs versus the only American survivor that hasn't relocated! Let's see how they stack up at the Tale of the Tape...

BUFFALO
TORONTO

WEATHER:
BUFFALO: Cold
TORONTO: Ninety northern miles colder, baby!
X ADVANTAGE: Sabres. Yes! I don't get to rub that in very often.

LOCAL KIDS WANT TO GROW UP TO BE:
BUFFALO: Employed
TORONTO: American
X ADVANTAGE: Sabres

ARE THERE ANY MISSPELLED WORDS IN THE NAMES OF THEIR ARENAS?:
BUFFALO: Marine Midland Arena. Lovely.
TORONTO: The Air Canada...Centre? What?
X ADVANTAGE: Sabres...not Sabers? Whoops.

GOALIE NICKNAMES:
BUFFALO: "The Dominator"—named after a movie you can get only in Amsterdam.
TORONTO: "Cujo"—named after the dog in a B movie.
X ADVANTAGE: Sabres

WHAT WE GOT FROM THEM:
BUFFALO: Well, Toronto gave us Doug Flutie.
TORONTO: Well, America gave us electricity, freedom, civilization...did I mention freedom?
X ADVANTAGE: Sabres

WHAT DO THEIR NAMES DO?:
SABRES: Slice
LEAFS: Fall
X ADVANTAGE: Sabres

HOW REGIONAL SNACKS AFFECT SCORING:
TORONTO: Tim Horton's doughnuts

BUFFALO: Wings!

ADVANTAGE: Sabres! I'll take the hot-scoring hand over a stay-at-home defenseman every time.

DO THEIR SOCKS HAVE STRIPES IN BANDS OF THREE?:

TORONTO: Yes

BUFFALO: Yes—no! Not part of the "new look."

ADVANTAGE: Sabres. Memo to the Maple Leafs: We cut the lollipop guild sketch!

FORCES OF DARKNESS:

TORONTO: Domi

BUFFALO: Satan. "Please allow me to introduce myself; I lit the lamp forty times this year."

ADVANTAGE: Sabres. Besides, I've always preferred the original Tie Domi—I believe they call him Rob Ray!

INSULTS THAT COULD CAUSE A DON-NYBROOK IN THE LOGE:

TORONTO: "Wide right, eh?"

BUFFALO: "Just be thankful we didn't trade you at Yalta for future considerations!"

ADVANTAGE: Push. Kids—no one wins when Mr. Hate comes a-calling!

BIG-TIME LOCAL MARKETING

BUFFALO: Flutie Flakes

TORONTO: Flutie Fluids...ohhh...

ADVANTAGE: Buffalo

WHAT LOCALS FERVENTLY WISH FOR:

BUFFALO: Lord Stanley's Cup

TORONTO: American TV

ADVANTAGE: Sabres

DISGRACE:

TORONTO: Fears of Quebec seceding

BUFFALO: The fact that Hasek went to Germany to consult a "soft tissue" specialist

ADVANTAGE: Push

TOOTH COUNT OF STARTING LINEUP:

TORONTO: 170 out of a possible 192

BUFFALO: 4 out of a possible 192. Now that's a play-off smile.

ADVANTAGE: Sabres

TRICK QUESTION: NUMBER OF SUPER BOWLS:

TORONTO: 0

BUFFALO: 4

ADVANTAGE: Buffalo! I knew the day would come when I could turn those losses into wins.

GREATEST ATHLETE:

BUFFALO: O. J. Simpson. Oh. Move on to the next one...

FAVORITE WAY TO GO OVER NIAGARA FALLS:

TORONTO: In a barrel

BUFFALO: In a muscle car

ADVANTAGE: Sabres

So there you have it; it's all so simple when you break things down sci-entifically. In a clanger off the crossbar, the advantage goes to Buffalo. But hang in there, Toronto—for some reason, you're still the only one with a Major League Baseball team. Until next time, I'm Nick Bakay, reminding you the numbers never lie.

By the way, the Sabres prevailed four games to one, and moved on to the Stanley Cup finals, where the Dallas Stars gave Buffalonians a reason to retire "Wide Right," and start living the dream otherwise known as "In the Crease."

As strange as it may sound in a world that has seen the Predators suc-ceed as an NHL franchise in the Deep South, there was a time when the now-mighty New Jersey Devils were rumored to be moving to what at the time seemed an improbable outpost...Nashville. Before the Devils became champs, the Nets became competitive, and Nashville learned to love the excitement that is icing, we took a look at the ramifications of relocation.

Great moments in New Jersey sports. Hmmm. Well, I guess we all remember that fabled night when Willis Reed hobbled onto the court...and begged Derrick Coleman to play defense. Now the No-Respect State is on the verge of watching a potential Stanley Cup champion blow town, for Nashville of all places. When it comes to good times, Tennessee rates hockey behind corn dogs and tractor pulls. What's next? The Martin Brodeur family theater in Branson, Missouri? All of a sudden I feel like Jeff Foxworthy: "If you think a Zamboni is something that tastes good with mustard, then you might be a redneck." But the beauty of sport is conflict: the Garden State vs. the Moonshine State. One fine hockey team, two potential homes. New Jersey, Nashville, let's see how they stack up at the Tale of the Tape.

CITY OR STATE:	STATE MOTTOES:
NEW JERSEY: State	NEW JERSEY: Perth Amboy at low tide: Priceless.
NASHVILLE: City	NASHVILLE: We isn't much on book learnin'!
X ADVANTAGE: Nashville. I hate teams named after vague geographic regions.	X ADVANTAGE: Jersey!

COLISEUM NAMES:
NEW JERSEY: The Brendan Byrne Arena
NASHVILLE: The Junior Samples Memorial Omniplex
ADVANTAGE: Nashville. A man so big, they had to bury him inside a municipal auditorium.

STADIUM FOOD FAVORITES:
NEW JERSEY: Pizza
NASHVILLE: Possum!
ADVANTAGE: Nashville. They say it "tastes like chicken."

TEAM SONGS:
NEW JERSEY: Here we go, Satan, here we go!
NASHVILLE: Theme from *Deliverance*
ADVANTAGE: Push...

DEFINITION OF "ICING":
NEW JERSEY: A hit by the Gambino crime family
NASHVILLE: The gooey stuff on top of a moon pie
ADVANTAGE: Push—there are no winners here.

BEST PLAYER:
NEW JERSEY: Martin Brodeur
NASHVILLE: Mr. Roy Clark
ADVANTAGE: Push

GREATEST MOMENT IN FRANCHISE HISTORY:
NASHVILLE DEVILS: The day they actually outdraw Travis Tritt
NEW JERSEY DEVILS: Schoenfeld to Koharski: "Have another doughnut, you fat pig!" Ah, that Noël Coward wit.
ADVANTAGE: Devils

STRATEGY:
NEW JERSEY: The Neutral Zone Trap
NASHVILLE: The Tush Push
ADVANTAGE: Push

A.K.A. :
NASHVILLE: Music City
NEW JERSEY: Sopranosylvania
ADVANTAGE: Uh, push

LOCAL FOOD CHAINS:
NEW JERSEY: Bill Parcells's Tuna Town Bistro
NASHVILLE: Chappy's Gravy Hutch—hot, steamin', and brown!
ADVANTAGE: Nashville

LOCAL FASHION:
NEW JERSEY: Shirts and shoes a must
NASHVILLE: An American classic—the "I'm with Stupid" T-shirt
ADVANTAGE: New Jersey

LOCALS ASPIRE TO BE:
NEW JERSEY: Teamsters
NASHVILLE: Organ donors
ADVANTAGE: Push

BIG-BODIED ENFORCERS:
NEW JERSEY: Scott Stevens
NASHVILLE: Wynonna
ADVANTAGE: Nashville!

So there you have it; it's all so simple when you break things down scientifically. In a wrist shot through the five hole, the advantage...goes to Nashville. Only time will tell how a banjo sounds playing "O Canada." Until next time, I'm Nick Bakay, reminding you the numbers never lie.

SAN FRANCISCO VS. NEW YORK

SAN FRANCISCO

NEW YORK

As teams, and towns, New York and San Francisco have a lot to offer, but when it comes to football, who has more? Niners versus Giants, The Big Apple versus the Left Coast, let's see how they stack up at the Tale of the Tape...

OCEANS:

SAN FRANCISCO: Where Barry Bonds buries milestone balls

NEW YORK: Where local mobsters bury rats

ADVANTAGE: Push. You'll never see best friends suing each other over the rights to a Gambino.

A.K.A. :

NEW YORK: The city that never sleeps

SAN FRANCISCO: The city that never sleeps with the opposite sex

ADVANTAGE: San Francisco—sex beats insomnia.

MOMENTS THAT WILL LIVE IN IGNOMINY:

SAN FRANCISCO: Terrell Owens gets jiggy with a Sharpie.

NEW YORK: Bret Favre lays down for Strahan.

ADVANTAGE: Push

THEIR TWO FAVORITE WORDS:

SAN FRANCISCO: "The Catch"

NEW YORK: "Wide Right"

ADVANTAGE: Oh, that smarts. Move on to the next one...

GOOD LUCK:

SAN FRANCISCO: Escaping Alcatraz

NEW YORK: Escaping anywhere at rush hour

ADVANTAGE: Push

THEY TAUGHT US HOW TO:

SAN FRANCISCO: Check off to the fourth receiver

NEW YORK: Start a white cornerback

ADVANTAGE: San Francisco

AHHH, THE SMELL OF IT!:

SAN FRANCISCO: The salty brine of Fisherman's Wharf

NEW YORK: The peculiar tang of a sub-way stairwell

ADVANTAGE: Push, and pass the Ozium.

SCREWING UP A GOOD THING:

NEW YORK: The "New" Times Square—Good-bye Peep World, Hello T.G.I. Friday's—this is progress?

SAN FRANCISCO: Sourdough bread—Hey, let's take a good thing and render it slightly bitter!

ADVANTAGE: Push

EDUCATIONAL NEIGHBORHOODS:

NEW YORK: Alphabet City

SAN FRANCISCO: The little-known Arithmetic Alley!

ADVANTAGE: Push. Gentrification coming soon!

MUSICAL:

NEW YORK: Broadway

SAN FRANCISCO: Journey!...Oof. The Grateful Dead! Oof...

ADVANTAGE: Push, and please pass the Zeppelin.

POETIC EPICENTERS:
SAN FRANCISCO: The City Lights Bookstore
NEW YORK: Any corner with someone off their meds
ADVANTAGE: Push. It's po-ems, who careth?

HILLS:
NEW YORK: Murray
SAN FRANCISCO: Nob
ADVANTAGE: Nob (wink!)

GOLDEN:
SAN FRANCISCO: Gate
NEW YORK: Palace—best Chinese on the Upper West Side!
ADVANTAGE: San Francisco

SUMMER OF:
SAN FRANCISCO: Love
NEW YORK: Sam
ADVANTAGE: San Francisco

QUAINT MODES OF TRANSPORTATION:
SAN FRANCISCO: The trolley
NEW YORK: Walking. I hear it's marvelous. In L.A. we drive to the bathroom.
ADVANTAGE: San Francisco

SEASONS:
NEW YORK: All four
SAN FRANCISCO: Fog
ADVANTAGE: NEW YORK

I:
...left my heart in San Francisco
...left my first wife in Times Square
ADVANTAGE: Push—both quite sad when you think about it.

CROONERS:
NEW YORK: Frank
SAN FRANCISCO: Tony
ADVANTAGE: New York...both guys are from there, right? Wrong! Sinatra and Bennett are from Jersey, just like the Giants, the Jets! In fact, there's only one football team that actually plays in the state of New York—ADVANTAGE: My Buffalo Bills! Talkin' proud, baby!

Ah, tennis. Today's top competitors are so young, I feel like I'm trapped at an Aaron Carter concert, yet I feel bad for these kids—a mere whiff of puberty, and it's back to oblivion. As long as privileged social climbers are willing to wait in line to watch country club brats battle for baseline bragging rights, however, the tradition will carry on. Case in point: the French Open and Wimbledon. Two big titles, two disparate cultures, let's see how they stack up at the Tale of the Tape.

STADIUM FOOD:
ENGLAND: Little bowls of strawberries and cream
FRANCE: Huge wheels of cheese so very stank
ADVANTAGE: The French Open

AMERICA'S FAVORITE CULTURAL ICON:
ENGLAND: Shakespeare
FRANCE: Pepe Le Pew
ADVANTAGE: Boy that's a tough one...England.

HOSPITALITY:
ENGLAND: Warm and friendly
FRANCE: Too busy sneering to remember that if it weren't for us, they'd be German.
ADVANTAGE: England

MUSICAL CONTRIBUTION:
ENGLAND: Led Zeppelin
FRANCE: The little songbird Edith Piaf...
ADVANTAGE: England

FOOD CONTRIBUTION:
FRENCH: Fries
ENGLISH: Muffins
ADVANTAGE: France

NATIONAL SPORTS:
ENGLAND: Rugby, soccer, darts
FRANCE: Sex
ADVANTAGE: France, in a squeaker

EVIDENCE OF EARLY INTELLIGENCE:
ENGLAND: Stonehenge
FRANCE: "Them garden slugs is *tres bien!*"
ADVANTAGE: Push...

ICONS OF MANLINESS:
ENGLAND: Beckham
FRANCE: Ummm...Depardieu?
ADVANTAGE: Push...

FOUGHT THE NAZIS:
ENGLAND: Yes
FRANCE: No
ADVANTAGE: England

DEEP THOUGHTS:
FRANCE: Existentialism
ENGLAND: Herman's Hermits
ADVANTAGE: Push. Herman's Hermits *embody* existentialism.

THE AMERICAN PHENOMENON THEY HAVE CHOSEN TO IGNORE:
ENGLAND: World League Football
FRANCE: Bathing
ADVANTAGE: England

WHEN AMERICA KICKED THEIR ASS:
FRANCE: 1803, The Louisiana Purchase—we bought the central time zone for the price of a decent second baseman.
ENGLAND: Seventeenth century, a little tea party called the Revolutionary War
ADVANTAGE: A little thing I like to call freedom, my friends.

So there you have it; it's so simple when you break things down scientifically. In a Chunnel buster, the advantage goes to England, and thereby Wimbledon. But don't feel bad for the French, this gives them a chance to indulge in their favorite indoor sport...sulking. Until next time, I'm Nick Bakay, reminding you the numbers never lie. Cheerio.

Back in the day, before anyone knew who Richard Jewel was, and seven years before Eric Robert Rudolph was apprehended while foraging in a Dumpster, Atlanta opened its arms to the 1996 Olympics—the first stateside games since those in L.A. For me, it raised the ultimate question: Which city would win in a street fight?

Atlanta has some mighty big shoes to fill as America's host body for the Olympic parasite. In 1984, Peter Ueberroth staged the Uber-games and Los Angeles set the bar for corporate sponsorship profit margins. Can Atlanta take the gold? The Left Coast versus the Deep South. Hollywood versus Tara. Stock the Olympic village with metal detectors, yak-blood smoothies, scores of politically motivated judges from nations that didn't even exist two years ago, and let's see how they stack up at the Tale of the Tape:

POPULATION:
ATLANTA: 3 million
LOS ANGELES: 9 million legal, so that means it's really hovering around 17 million
[X] ADVANTAGE: Atlanta

CITY IS KNOWN FOR:
ATLANTA: Peach pies
LOS ANGELES: Drive-bys
[X] ADVANTAGE: Atlanta

MOST POPULAR MALE NAME:
ATLANTA: Beauregard
LOS ANGELES: Jesus
[– –] ADVANTAGE: Push

WE HAVE THESE CITIES TO THANK FOR:
ATLANTA: The glory days of John Rocker
LOS ANGELES: Breast implants
[X] ADVANTAGE: Los Angeles

HOME OF:
ATLANTA: The Center for Disease Control and Prevention
LOS ANGELES: The center for disease
[X] ADVANTAGE: Atlanta

LOCAL LANDMARKS:
LOS ANGELES: The Hustler Store—Your one-stop supershop for lattes and lube
ATLANTA: The Ray Lewis parking lot
[X] ADVANTAGE: Los Angeles

LUCKY TOURISTS MAY SEE:
ATLANTA: Pamela Anderson
LOS ANGELES: NBA stars trolling at The Gold Club
[X] ADVANTAGE: Los Angeles

NFL FRANCHISE:
ATLANTA: Falcons
LOS ANGELES: None
[X] ADVANTAGE: Los Angeles. No blackouts! We can see Michael Vick *every* Sunday.

LOCAL INDUSTRY:
ATLANTA: Corn
LOS ANGELES: Porn
[– –] ADVANTAGE: Push

NAME MEANS:
ATLANTA: Greek goddess who joined Caledonian boar hunt. Sort of a Pam Postema thing...
LOS ANGELES: Spanish for "The Angels"
[X] ADVANTAGE: La La Land

So there you have it; it's so simple when you break things down scientifically. In a Dream team–Micronesia landslide, the advantage goes to Los Angeles. But hang in there, ATL—at least you aren't the home of smog, earthquakes, riots, landslides, floods, or Tom Arnold. Until next time, I'm Nick Bakay, reminding you the numbers never lie.

Institutions

EXTREME GAMES

THE OLYMPICS

The Extreme Games: renegade events that are being invented as we speak. No owners, no strikes, no personal seat licenses, just pre-*Jackass* thrill-seekers gettin' their freak on. How does this counterculture jocka-palooza compare to the granddaddy of them all—the Olympic Games? Let's see how they stack up at the Tale of the Tape.

IF THE ATHLETES ARE PRECARIOUSLY AIRBORNE:
OLYMPICS: Something has gone terribly wrong
EXTREME GAMES: Aw-right!
ADVANTAGE: Extreme Games

OPENING CEREMONIES:
OLYMPICS: The lighting of the torch
EXTREME GAMES: The lighting of the bong
ADVANTAGE: Push...and may neither be extinguished.

OFFICIAL CANDY BAR:
OLYMPICS: Whoever won the product placement war
EXTREME GAMES: Dr. Bronner's Environmentally Safe, Cruelty-Free Carob and Yogurt Globs
ADVANTAGE: Olympics

BIGGEST SELLING POINT:
OLYMPICS: The nations of the world compete
EXTREME GAMES: No Dick Button!
ADVANTAGE: Extreme Games

ECO-CHALLENGE:
EXTREME GAMES: An event
OLYMPICS: The Port-O-Potties
ADVANTAGE: Extreme Games

THE ONLY PEOPLE WITH THE POWER TO BOYCOTT:
OLYMPICS: The president
EXTREME GAMES: Avril Lavigne
ADVANTAGE: Push...

HUMAN INTEREST PROFILES:
OLYMPICS: Up Close and Personal
EXTREME GAMES: Up Tight and Grody
ADVANTAGE: Extreme Games

THE ATHLETES ARE HOUSED AT:
OLYMPICS: The Olympic Village
EXTREME GAMES: The Biosphere
ADVANTAGE: Extreme Games

WINNERS GO TO:
OLYMPICS: The White House
EXTREME GAMES: The Zima factory
ADVANTAGE: Push!

BEST SPECTATOR VANTAGE POINT:
OLYMPICS: The seats
EXTREME GAMES: The mosh pit
ADVANTAGE: Extreme Games

POPULAR CHANTS:
OLYMPICS: USA! USA!
EXTREME GAMES: Duuuuuude!
ADVANTAGE: Olympics

FIRST PRIZE:
OLYMPICS: Gold medals
EXTREME GAMES: Brass balls
ADVANTAGE: Push...

INNER MONOLOGUE:
OLYMPICS: "I will stay focused."
EXTREME GAMES: "Did I remember to tape *Crank Yankers*?"
ADVANTAGE: Extreme Games

AFFIRMATIONS ATHLETES POST IN THEIR ROOMS:
OLYMPICS: Never surrender; never give up.
EXTREME GAMES: Employees must wash hands.
ADVANTAGE: Extreme Games

OFFICIAL STATIONERY:
OLYMPICS: Five-ring Olympic logo
EXTREME GAMES: The little laughing cartoon guy saying, "You want it when?"
ADVANTAGE: Extreme Games

WHAT THE ATHLETES KEEP FOR THE REST OF THEIR LIVES:
OLYMPICS: The pride of having been an Olympian
EXTREME GAMES: A new plastic knee
ADVANTAGE: Push

So there you have it; it's so simple when you break things down scientifically. In a spine-be-damned triple flip, the advantage goes to the Extreme Games. All I can say is good luck, have a ball, and go easy on the Red Bull. Until next time, I'm Nick Bakay, reminding you the numbers never lie.

BASEBALL VS. CHURCH

National pastime, or time with a pastor? This is the question. Whether 'tis better to play or pray has weighed heavily on the hearts of man, especially on Sundays. Let us now awaken our souls and open our hearts as we compare these two genteel activities at the Tale of the Tape:

UH-OH:
BASEBALL: Your best player tests positive...again.
CHURCH: Father Joe is led away in handcuffs...again.
X ADVANTAGE: Baseball

MILLIONS:
BASEBALL: In signing bonuses
CHURCH: In hush money
X ADVANTAGE: Baseball

DISTRACTIONS:
BASEBALL: Seventh-inning stretch
CHURCH: The hottie on the left with the new annulment
X ADVANTAGE: Church

HOLLOWED:
BASEBALL: Sammy Sosa's bat
CHURCH: Your hymnal, to accommodate some cheese to go with that wine
X ADVANTAGE: Church

KNOWN TO CAUSE:
BASEBALL: Couch potatoism
CHURCH: War
X ADVANTAGE: Baseball

FALL GUYS:
CHURCH: Satan
BASEBALL: Buckner
X ADVANTAGE: Church. Hard to beat a red, scaly tail.

CROWD-PLEASING GIMMICKS:
BASEBALL: The Rally Monkey
CHURCH: The Rally Monk
X ADVANTAGE: Baseball. Again, hard to beat a tail.

SPECIALISTS:
BASEBALL: Left-handed relief pitchers
CHURCH: Exorcists
X ADVANTAGE: Church. Never saw a movie about a left-handed relief pitcher...

THE SHOW:
BASEBALL: Making the big leagues
CHURCH: Making heaven
X ADVANTAGE: Baseball. No signing bonuses in heaven...

LATIN:
CHURCH: Old masses
BASEBALL: Young infielders
X ADVANTAGE: Baseball

ACCESSORIES:
BASEBALL: Big swinging necklace with your player's number on it
CHURCH: Big swinging purse smokin' with frankincense
-- ADVANTAGE: Push. No winners here.

HEAD GEAR:
BASEBALL: Cap, batting helmet
CHURCH: Tall enough to hide a small boy
X ADVANTAGE: Baseball

WHERE THE BIG MOMENT IS REPLAYED:
BASEBALL: Diamond Vision
CHURCH: Stained glass
X ADVANTAGE: Baseball

THE FALL CLASSIC:
BASEBALL: World Series
CHURCH: Adam chomps apple
X ADVANTAGE: Baseball

MUSIC:
BASEBALL: Organ
CHURCH: Organ
– – ADVANTAGE: Push

BARELY TOLERATED:
BASEBALL: Rain delays
CHURCH: Vain displays
X ADVANTAGE: Church

SACRIFICES:
BASEBALL: Flies
CHURCH: Lambs, virgins, et al.
X ADVANTAGE: Baseball

PRICE OF ADMISSION:
BASEBALL: $10.00-$60.00
CHURCH: Loose change, and one guilty soul
X ADVANTAGE: Church

CUISINE:
BASEBALL: Wieners and beer
CHURCH: Wafers and wine
X ADVANTAGE: Baseball, in a close one

BIG BIRDS:
BASEBALL: Cardinals
CHURCH: Cardinals
– – ADVANTAGE: Push

DISTINCTIVE ODORS:
BASEBALL: New seats
CHURCH: Old pews
X ADVANTAGE: Baseball

CROWD ACTIVITIES:
BASEBALL: Praying
CHURCH: Praying
– – ADVANTAGE: Push

MOST DREADED ACTIVITY:
CHURCH: Confession
BASEBALL: Concession
X ADVANTAGE: Church

MOST POPULAR NAME:
CHURCH: Jesus
BASEBALL: Jesus
– – ADVANTAGE: Push

NO-NO:
BASEBALL: Spitball
CHURCH: Punish the Pope
X ADVANTAGE: Baseball

So there you have it; as predicted, when you break things down scientifically, nine men defeat a-men and the house that Ruth built appears to stand taller than that of the Lord...at least until Steinbrenner lures him to the Yankees. Until next time, I'm Nick Bakay, reminding you the numbers never lie.

GRADUATION
OZZFEST

You can blow a save any time, but how often does Black Sabbath get back together? Apparently that was John Rocker's logic the year he chose flying to Atlanta for Ozzfest over a controversy-free start with the Cleveland Indians. The fact that it happened the same week Vince Carter chose to grab his diploma over sinking a series-winning jumper in the play-offs pushed athletes and their off days into the spotlight.

Now, on the surface it would appear more valid to squeeze your commencement in between games than to blow a save because your ears are still ringing from the twelfth encore. Then again, Rocker took his chances on a regular season game, while Carter rolled the dice with the season on the line. So, it's time to get to the bottom of extracurricular risk versus reward: attending your graduation, attending Ozzfest. Who really had the best destination? Let's see how they stack up at the Tale of the Tape.

YOUR BIG MOMENT:
GRADUATION: The school president hands you your diploma.
OZZFEST: Ozzy hands you a flailing headless dove.
ADVANTAGE: Graduation, unless the parchment is infectious. X

TOSS:
GRADUATION: Your cap
OZZFEST: Your cookies
ADVANTAGE: Graduation

ANDROGYNOUS OPENING ACTS:
GRADUATION: The Whiffenpoofs
OZZFEST: Marilyn Manson
ADVANTAGE: Ozzfest X

HYPOCRISY:
GRADUATION: The university awards an honorary doctorate to a celebrity with a ninth-grade education.
OZZFEST: Ozzy urges you all to drive home safely.
ADVANTAGE: Push

EMOTIONAL MOMENTS:
GRADUATION: Your parents realize they just spent $120,000 so you could learn how to tap a keg.
OZZFEST: Since when did Black Sabbath feature Kelly Osbourne?
ADVANTAGE: Push

CLIQUES:
GRADUATION: Phi Beta Kappa
OZZFEST: I Phelta Thi
ADVANTAGE: Ozzfest

ENCORES:
GRADUATION: "Pomp and Circumstance"
OZZFEST: "War Pigs"
ADVANTAGE: Ozzfest

THE BIG THREE:
GRADUATION: Reading, writing, arithmetic
OZZFEST: Sex, drugs, and Rock 'n Roll
ADVANTAGE: Ozzfest. In the current political climate, S,D,R&R are better qualifications if you want to be elected president.

MEMORIES:
GRADUATION: In your heart for a lifetime
OZZFEST: In your bloodstream for a week
ADVANTAGE: Graduation

THE MORNING AFTER:
GRADUATION: You wake up to the reality of no job and massive student loan debt.
OZZFEST: You wake up to the reality of a skinhead spooning you in the drunk tank.
ADVANTAGE: Push!

"OH, DEAR!":
GRADUATION: The valedictorian considers his speech one last chance to kiss teachers' butts.
OZZFEST: The mosh pit is sponsored by Zima.
ADVANTAGE: Push

SECOND STAGE:
GRADUATION: A humble barbecue for the kids who finished a few credits short.
OZZFEST: A little stage with bands no one has heard of.
ADVANTAGE: Push

CLICHÉS:
GRADUATION: "You are the leaders of tomorrow..."
OZZFEST: "Hello, Atlanta!"
ADVANTAGE: Push

So there you have it; it's so simple when you break things down scientifically. In a race that finished tighter than Rocker's Shea Stadium security, the advantage goes to...push!

I guess I'm in favor of any individual who chooses to let his freak flag fly in the face of conventional wisdom. That being said, I remain confident Rocker will continue to give me a reason to regret this. Until next time, I'm Nick Bakay, reminding you the numbers never lie.

SUPER BOWL | **SURVIVOR**

In an era of audience fragmentation, the Super Bowl may be the only national holiday we still agree on. Miss it, and you can expect to be stoned to death outside a Costco. Indeed, you should be stoned to death...maybe the Costco part is overkill. Ironically, the big game now shares its hype with a show rife with parasites: the much anticipated premier of *Survivor*. In the big picture, *Survivor* may be a mere blip on our pop-culture radar, but it will be sharing center stage on every TV set in the land. Which begs the question: Which one will generate the most Monday-morning quarterbacking? Super Bowl, *Survivor*, let's see how they stack up at the Tale of the Tape...

LIFE EXPECTANCY:
SUPER BOWL: Eternal
SURVIVOR: 'Til some contestant gets monkey pox
ADVANTAGE: Super Bowl

THINGS YOU CAN NEVER UN-SEE:
SUPER BOWL: Tony Siragusa, postshower and just as God intended him
SURVIVOR: Hatch's hang-down
ADVANTAGE: Push, and give me a second here so I can stab out my eyes.

RISKS YOU RUN
SUPER BOWL: For the rest of your life, your new middle name could be "wide right."
SURVIVOR: Insects could lay eggs in your open wounds.
ADVANTAGE: Push

ANNUAL MIGRATIONS:
SUPER BOWL: Tampa, Miami, New Orleans
SURVIVOR: Fiji, Australia, Syndication
ADVANTAGE: Super Bowl, until *Survivor* sends tribes to Bourbon Street without any Zantac.

SHAME:
SUPER BOWL: You're the first player busted in a red-light district the night before the game.
SURVIVOR: You're voted off the island for hoarding Snickers.
ADVANTAGE: Push

MVPS:
SUPER BOWL: "I'm going to Disneyland!"
SURVIVOR: "I found some kick-ass wiping leaves!"
ADVANTAGE: Super Bowl

HARD TO WATCH:
SUPER BOWL: The halftime show
SURVIVOR: The ketosis
ADVANTAGE: Push

DON'T TURN YOUR BACK ON:
SUPER BOWL: Ray Lewis
SURVIVOR: The chick who drives a truck
ADVANTAGE: Push

WE REALLY NEED:
SUPER BOWL: A first down!
SURVIVOR: Ointment!
ADVANTAGE: Super Bowl

GET USED TO SEX WITH:
SUPER BOWL: The inevitable undercover vice cop
SURVIVOR: The cameras rolling
ADVANTAGE: Push

LONELINESS IS:
SUPER BOWL: Finding yourself two steps behind an all-pro receiver
SURVIVOR: Finding your swimsuit area covered in a strange, aggressive rash
ADVANTAGE: Super Bowl

WHICH GUMBEL YOU GET TO MEET:
SUPER BOWL: Greg
SURVIVOR: Bryant
ADVANTAGE: Super Bowl

GAME PLANS:
SUPER BOWL: Prey on the old and the weak.
SURVIVOR: Build an alliance to prey on the old and the weak.
ADVANTAGE: Push

RECORDS:
SUPER BOWL: Your defense allowed the fewest points.
SURVIVOR: Your tribe had the fewest solid bowel movements.
ADVANTAGE: Super Bowl

So there you have it; it's all so simple when you break things down scientifically: In a tribal council meeting in full pads, the advantage goes to the Super Bowl. But hang in there, *Survivor*, you can stay warm by the fire of your exorbitant ad rates. Until next time, I'm Nick Bakay, reminding you the numbers never lie.

SPORTS
WAR

They say sport is the civilized man's war. On the eve of what will probably be my last millennium (unless all this Ginsana kicks in), I'm prone to ponder: Is it? As we pray for peace in the next century, it's time to put it to the test: Letter Men versus MPs, hardware versus hardball. War. Sports. Let's see how they stack up at the Tale of the Tape...

OBJECTIVE:
SPORTS: To dominate for four quarters
WAR: To dominate the Earth, and split it into four quarters, all named after you
X ADVANTAGE: War. I love a big thinker.

TRAINING:
SPORTS: A lifetime of reps, weights, and aerobics
WAR: Six months of rebuilding your mental desktop to recognize that you are the sub-human, sub-military slime they keep saying you are
X ADVANTAGE: My wife tells me that. War.

GRACE UNDER FIRE:
SPORTS: Showing poise in the pocket
WAR: Leaving a couple of buildings standing
X ADVANTAGE: Sports

PLAY-OFF TICKETS:
SPORTS: A few grand apiece
WAR: A billion dollars per country
X ADVANTAGE: Sports

GIMMICKS AND STUNTS:
SPORTS: A fan shoots a free throw from midcourt for a scholarship
WAR: The marines help the locals knock down a mammoth statue of the ex-dictator
X ADVANTAGE: War

DECISION MAKERS:
SPORTS: Coaches, managers, owners
WAR: Whoever sits closer to the no-dial red phone
X ADVANTAGE: Sports

AIR TRANSPORTATION:
SPORTS: Fully staffed charter jet with attractive stewardesses, roomy leather seating, and Starbucks coffee
WAR: C-16 military aircraft, no luggage handlers, no seats, flowing vomit gutters
X ADVANTAGE: Sports

PERKS:
SPORTS: Women, fortune, and fame
WAR: You can off your enemies
- - ADVANTAGE: Oooh, that's a push.

HOW TO GET IN:
SPORTS: Have the ability to do something cool with a ball.
WAR: Prove your feet aren't flat, sign your name.
X ADVANTAGE: War

GET ME OUT OF HERE:
SPORTS: Your trade to the Canucks just cost you a 30 percent tax hike.
WAR: Wait a minute—these guys think they get *virgins* if they die?!
- - ADVANTAGE: Push

TODAY'S DATE:
SPORTS: Supermodels and actresses
WAR: A librarian in Manila, and a mother-daughter thing in the South Pacific
– – ADVANTAGE: Push?

WHEN:
SPORTS: Seasonal
WAR: Perennial
X ADVANTAGE: Sports

LOCATION, LOCATION, LOCATION:
SPORTS: In stadiums all over the world
WAR: In countries all over the world who just don't get the human rights thing
– – ADVANTAGE: Push

HAUNTING THOUGHTS:
SPORTS: "Does this town have a Hooters?"
WAR: "The USO is sending Carmen Electra. I'm gonna offer her my burrito."
X ADVANTAGE: Sports

PRICE GOUGING:
SPORTS: The IOC—more free dinners than Tommy Lasorda
WAR: The Pentagon—more $90 screwdrivers than a strip club
– – ADVANTAGE: Push

ACTS OF SURRENDER:
WAR: Wave a white flag
SPORTS: Start Akili Smith
X ADVANTAGE: War

AIN'T NO WAY TO TREAT A LADY:
SPORTS: "With the fifth selection, the St. Louis Rams pick...Lawrence Phillips!"
WAR: "Welcome to Tail Hook, ladies!"
– – ADVANTAGE: Push—there are no winners here.

DON'T ASK, DON'T TELL:
SPORTS: "Oh, it's just some homeopathic thing that helps aerate my muscles."
WAR: "Sarge...are these yours?!"
– – ADVANTAGE: Push

RETALIATION:
SPORTS: Purpose pitch
WAR: Shock and awe
X ADVANTAGE: War

PUSHOVERS:
SPORTS: The Clippers
WAR: Grenada
X ADVANTAGE: War, in a squeaker

RIVALRIES:
SPORTS: OSU vs. Michigan
WAR: Us vs. Them
X ADVANTAGE: War

BRAIN TEASERS:
SPORTS: Solving the triangle offense
WAR: Wait a sec—they don't *want* to take off the veils?
X ADVANTAGE: War

So there you have it; in a blitzkrieg, the advantage goes to push. And not because there are no winners here but because there are no losers. Most men would do it over to be a sports star if they possibly could, but if it weren't for the true warriors, no one would even have that opportunity. And Lord knows I'd rather fight for this team than some cuckoo-for-soccerpuffs, kick-the-can country. Until next time, I'm Nick Bakay, reminding you the numbers never lie.

NASCAR YACHTING

The America's Cup? All I can say about a sport where men compete in khaki shorts is how hasn't this caught on in the inner city? High-stakes yachting is an event best described using a Thurston Howell III voice: "I simply *adore* Labrador Retrievers!" Maybe that's why the good Lord made NASCAR. It's loud, it's dangerous, it's accessible to the working man, and you best believe there's gonna be a little contact! But is it that simple? Am I doing the elitist magic of yachting a grave disservice? Let's see how they stack up at the Tale of the Tape...

WHERE STARS MET THEIR WIVES:
NASCAR: The Texarkana Hooters
YACHTING: Her coming out party
X ADVANTAGE: NASCAR

RELATABILITY:
NASCAR: We all drive cars.
YACHTING: How many own a yacht?
Show of hands...
X ADVANTAGE: NASCAR

WHAT THEY CALL THEIR GROUPIES:
NASCAR: Pit lizards
YACHTING: Sail sluts
- - ADVANTAGE: Push. Everyone wins with groupies.

WINNER'S CIRCLE BEVERAGE OF CHOICE:
NASCAR: Suds, brew
YACHTING: Champers, bubbly
- - ADVANTAGE: Push

	HOW THEY GO FAST:		**REQUIREMENTS:**
X	NASCAR: Drop the hammer YACHTING: Unfurl the topsail ADVANTAGE: NASCAR	X	NASCAR: 'Nads the size of cantaloupes YACHTING: Money ADVANTAGE: NASCAR
– –	**WHEN YOUR VEHICLE IS REALLY FLYING:** NASCAR: Jack the bear! YACHTING: My, she's yahr! ADVANTAGE: Push—both are too oblique.	– –	**SPONSORS:** NASCAR: Tobacco YACHTING: Privilege ADVANTAGE: Push
X	**THINGS CAN GET UGLY WHEN YOU:** NASCAR: Slap the wall YACHTING: Scuff your Topsiders ADVANTAGE: NASCAR	– –	**SCANDALS:** NASCAR: Jeff Gordon's divorce YACHTING: The Skipper, Gilligan, and the poop deck ADVANTAGE: Push
X	**BOSUN'S CHAIR:** NASCAR: That halter top Miss Fram Oil Filter is spilling out of YACHTING: A canvas seat used to hoist someone up the mast ADVANTAGE: NASCAR		

So there you have it; in an oily skid mark, the checkered flag goes to NASCAR. But keep your head held high, all you able seamen—at least you don't spend your weekends ballooning. Until next time, I'm Nick Bakay, reminding you the numbers never lie.

Political conventions and the Olympics: Both take a decent principle and pimp it out as though they're working the streets like Willy Dynamite. They also take forgone conclusions and drag them out for the sake of filling TV airtime. Do we really care? Let's see how they stack up at the Tale of the Tape.

HOT-BUTTON ISSUES:
POLITICAL CONVENTION: Abortion
OLYMPICS: Aborted attempts at creating a level playing field between the USA and Nowashistan
ADVANTAGE: Push

INHERENT PROBLEMS:
POLITICAL CONVENTION: The Democrat is inevitably dull, the Republican is inevitably a mongoloid rich kid.
OLYMPICS: Every four years we are forced to learn the name of some dude who runs really fast. Not to catch a ball, or to steal home, just runs real, real fast!
ADVANTAGE: Push

DONKEY:
POLITICAL CONVENTION: Symbolic of the Democratic Party
OLYMPICS: Thanks to sports medicine, the current DNA structure of China's women's track team
ADVANTAGE: Push

BLATANT SIGNS OF CORRUPTION:
POLITICAL CONVENTION: Handguns now classified as an agricultural product.
OLYMPICS: The Slovakian judge locked her bread line pass in the trunk of her new Porsche.
ADVANTAGE: Push

THE CROWD:
POLITICAL CONVENTION: Nut bags with paper hats and signs
OLYMPICS: Nut bags with passports, paper hats, and signs
ADVANTAGE: Push

FLAGS:
POLITICAL CONVENTION: Something to drape the lies in
OLYMPICS: Something to filter the steroids out of your pee
ADVANTAGE: Push

SOMETHING YOU CAN DEPEND ON:
POLITICAL CONVENTION: Dull speeches
OLYMPICS: Dull 2A.M. fireside chat wrap-ups
ADVANTAGE: Push

DURING THE NATIONAL ANTHEM:
POLITICAL CONVENTION: Candidates scan the room for fresh intern talent.
OLYMPICS: Cubans scan the room for exit signs.
ADVANTAGE: Push

UNBEATABLE RECORDS:
POLITICAL CONVENTION: In '92, Clinton copped 604 feels on his way to the podium.
OLYMPICS: In '96, the Dream Team impregnated 4,312 women.
ADVANTAGE: Push—there's untouchable, and then there's touch 'em all!

THE OLYMPICS VS. POLITICAL CONVENTIONS

THE LIGHTING OF THE TORCH:
POLITICAL CONVENTION: How nervous politicos handle prespeech gas
OLYMPICS: What the snowboarding team calls firing up the bong
ADVANTAGE: Push

BRIBES:
POLITICAL CONVENTION: The best way to become a cabinet member
OLYMPICS: The best way to guarantee your city gets to host the games
ADVANTAGE: Push

MORTAL LOCKS:
POLITICAL CONVENTION: Ted Kennedy will sober up long enough to make us forget they made their fortune bootlegging.
OLYMPICS: A Dream Team will pummel a third-world country decimated by a hot-zone virus.
ADVANTAGE: Push

NAMES THAT WON'T COME UP:
POLITICAL CONVENTION: J. Edgar Hoover's dressmaker
OLYMPICS: The best lay in the Olympic village
ADVANTAGE: Push

BIG GALS WITH A GREAT ATTITUDE:
POLITICAL CONVENTION: Monica Lewinsky
OLYMPICS: The shot-putter on the German women's team who has testicles she calls "Das Boys"
ADVANTAGE: Push

A GREAT EXCUSE TO BUY:
POLITICAL CONVENTION: A vote in Congress
OLYMPICS: TiVo
ADVANTAGE: Push

So there you have it; in an electoral landslide, the advantage goes to push. Personally, I'll just take the vig and pretend none of this ever happened. However, if I had my druthers, I'd cancel both and attend something clean and pure...like a cock fight. Until next time, I'm Nick Bakay, reminding you the numbers never lie.

What does it say about our collective 'naddage when the majority of us continually mark the month of May by ignoring the balls-out mayhem that is NHL play-off action? And for what, the eye-watering yawn of baseball players shaking off-season rust? The NBA play-offs, which reach critical mass only during the hour it takes to run off the final forty-five seconds and you get a foul for *nudging* someone? Desperate times call for desperate measures, so it's come to this: In a feeble attempt to make the Western final matchup of the Wild versus the Mighty Ducks more relatable to a *soft* populace, it's time to approach Anaheim and Bloomington from a different angle: tourist attractions. The Mall of America, which draws 42 million visitors every year, versus the original family destination, Disneyland. Let's see how they stack up at the Tale of the Tape...

THEY CLAIM TO BE:
MALL OF AMERICA: The largest *fully enclosed* retail and entertainment complex in America
DISNEYLAND: The happiest place on Earth
ADVANTAGE: Disneyland. Is fully enclosed such a good thing? **[X]**

SWEET JESUS!:
MALL OF AMERICA: They've got a J. Crew *right next to* a Banana Republic!
DISNEYLAND: They opened a Spearmint Rhino in Downtown Disney!
ADVANTAGE: Disneyland **[X]**

THE BEST PLACE TO:
MALL OF AMERICA: Get run over in the parking lot by Randy Moss
DISNEYLAND: See old Rally Monkeys panhandling
ADVANTAGE: Push **[- -]**

SANITIZED METAPHORS:
MALL OF AMERICA: Weiner-on-a-stick
DISNEYLAND: The only Main Street, USA, devoid of pungent schizophrenics off their meds
ADVANTAGE: Mall of America **[X]**

BEWARE WHEN:
MALL OF AMERICA: Kirby Puckett follows you into the bathroom.
DISNEYLAND: Michael Jackson rents out the entire park, just for the two of you.
ADVANTAGE: Push, and pass the pepper spray. **[- -]**

OFTEN HEARD:
MALL OF AMERICA: Man, this was a long way to drive just to see *another* Sharper Image.
DISNEYLAND: Becky, sweetie, don't punch Goofy *there*...
ADVANTAGE: Disneyland **[X]**

ALTERED STATES:
MALL OF AMERICA: A contact-high from the noxious perfume they pump out of Victoria's Secret
DISNEYLAND: Mommy and Daddy discover Bloody Mary Land.
ADVANTAGE: Disneyland **[X]**

INNER MONOLOGUES:

MALL OF AMERICA: "Maybe if I buy *this*, I'll finally be happy."

DISNEYLAND: "*My* parents never took me anywhere."

- - ADVANTAGE: Push

ANTHROPOMORPHIZED GODHEADS:

MALL OF AMERICA: Snoopy

DISNEYLAND: Mickey

- - ADVANTAGE: Push. The rest of you see them too, right?

NEW ADDITIONS:

MALL OF AMERICA: Gap Ghetto Fabulous

DISNEYLAND: Miramax Island: Must be 17, or accompanied by a guardian

- - ADVANTAGE: Push

SIDE EFFECTS:

MALL OF AMERICA: Your Visa card hasn't been this maxed out since that ill-advised visit to the Gold Club VIP room.

DISNEYLAND: Every time you hear "It's a Small World After All," you weep uncontrollably.

X ADVANTAGE: Mall of America

I GET TWO WEEKS OFF A YEAR, AND I HAVE TO SPEND IT:

MALL OF AMERICA: Waiting for my wife outside a shoe store

DISNEYLAND: Looking for the smoking area in "Pooh's Home"

- - ADVANTAGE: Push

LOCAL HOCKEY TEAMS ARE NAMED AFTER:

MALL OF AMERICA: Um...nature?

DISNEYLAND: The end of Emilio Estevez's career

X ADVANTAGE: Mall of America

So there you have it; it's all so simple when you break things down scientifically. In a squeaker, the advantage goes to Disneyland, but hang in there, you big, bodacious mall, I'm sure it's nothing a Disney Store couldn't solve. Until next time, I'm Nick Bakay, reminding you the numbers never lie.

INDIANAPOLIS 500
THE KENTUCKY DERBY

The need to go fast is an American birthright, and May is the month for the two biggest races of the year: the Kentucky Derby and the Indianapolis 500. But which one really deserves to be called the Big Daddy of American horsepower? Gasoline Alley vs. the thunder of the backstretch, Churchill Downs versus the Brickyard, let's see how they stack up at the Tale of the Tape.

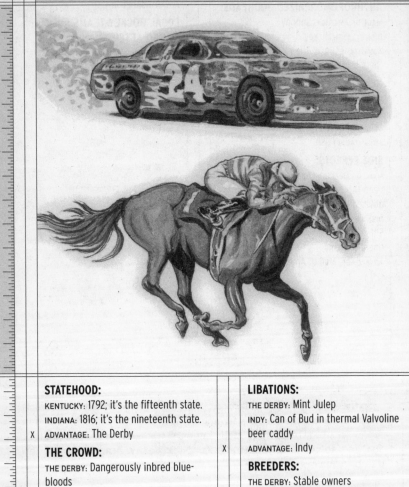

STATEHOOD:
KENTUCKY: 1792; it's the fifteenth state.
INDIANA: 1816; it's the nineteenth state.
X ADVANTAGE: The Derby

THE CROWD:
THE DERBY: Dangerously inbred blue-bloods
INDY: Dangerously inbred hicks
– ADVANTAGE: Push

LIBATIONS:
THE DERBY: Mint Julep
INDY: Can of Bud in thermal Valvoline beer caddy
X ADVANTAGE: Indy

BREEDERS:
THE DERBY: Stable owners
INDY: The women in the bleachers
X ADVANTAGE: The Derby

POPULATION MARRIED TO OTHER FAMILY MEMBERS:
INDY: Zero
DERBY: 42 Percent
X ADVANTAGE: Kentucky

TYPICAL STADIUM ATTIRE:
THE DERBY: Designer fashion
INDY: "I'm with Stupid" T-shirts
X ADVANTAGE: The Derby

UNIFORM:
INDY RACERS: Futuristic Devo jumpsuits with helmets that can withstand the impact of a speeding meteor
DERBY JOCKEYS: Clothing borrowed from the Lollypop Guild
X ADVANTAGE: The Indy 500

OWNERS' WIVES ENJOY:
INDY: The exhilaration of driving really fast
THE DERBY: The stable boys
-- ADVANTAGE: Push

RACE'S NICKNAME:
KENTUCKY DERBY: The run for the roses
INDY 500: The drive in circles 'til you hurl
X ADVANTAGE: The Derby

TAILGATE PARTIES:
KENTUCKY DERBY: Cocktails at the Governor's Ball
INDY 500: Corn dogs and a kegger
X ADVANTAGE: The Derby

THE WINNER GETS TO:
INDY 500: Hang out with some blondes in the winner's circle.
THE DERBY: Stand stud for the next twenty years.
X ADVANTAGE: The Derby!

So there you have it; it's all so simple when you break things down scientifically. The winner, by a nose, is the Kentucky Derby. But hang in there, Indiana; you've still got Bobby Knight…oops! Until next time, I'm Nick Bakay, reminding you the numbers never lie.

ROCK 'N' ROLL VS. SPORTS

It's time to raise a glass to our two greatest exports: sports and Rock 'n' Roll. At a time when you can fire up your satellite dish and jump from the Barcelona Dragons to a Japanese Elvis impersonator, the one salient truth of our global village is underscored: You're either American, or you want to be. Hell, even the French would trade their insolent baguettes for one night as James Brown. But which cultural force really deserves to be crowned king? Let's see how they stack up at the Tale of the Tape...

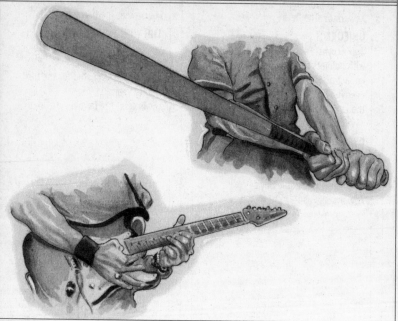

GROIN PULLS:
SPORTS: A problem
ROCK 'N' ROLL: An objective
ADVANTAGE: Rock 'n' Roll

ENCORES:
SPORTS: Tear down the goal posts
ROCK 'N' ROLL: Hold up a lighter
ADVANTAGE: Sports

BEST NAMES:
SPORTS: Magic Johnson
ROCK 'N' ROLL: Sex Pistols
ADVANTAGE: Push, with a tip of the hat to Limp Bizkit.

WORST NAMES:
SPORTS: Baltimore Ravens
ROCK 'N' ROLL: Spandau Ballet
ADVANTAGE: Sports. I hate Modell, but not as much as a band that calls itself *that*.

ROCK 'N' ROLL VS. SPORTS

LEWD LOGOS:
SPORTS: The old Buccaneers guy
ROCK 'N' ROLL: The Stones' tongue
X ADVANTAGE: Sports. At least the Buccaneers guy knew when to retire.

WHAT YOU'LL NEVER HEAR:
SPORTS: The kicker got fined for helmet-to-helmet contact.
ROCK 'N' ROLL: The trombone player locked his keys in his Porsche.
X ADVANTAGE: Sports

METAPHORICALLY:
SPORTS: Civilized war
ROCK 'N' ROLL: Civilized sex
– – ADVANTAGE: Push. Throw in some corn dogs and we've got a party.

PROTECTION:
SPORTS: Cup
ROCK 'N' ROLL: Codpiece
X ADVANTAGE: Sports

STANDARD PARAMEDIC EQUIPMENT:
SPORTS: Halo brace
ROCK 'N' ROLL: Stomach pump
– – ADVANTAGE: Push—there are no winners here.

WORST TRADES:
SPORTS: The '90's Dallas Cowboys for Herschel Walker
ROCK 'N' ROLL: David Lee Roth for Sammy Hagar
X ADVANTAGE: Sports

WHO GOES TOPLESS?:
SPORTS: Ugly painted men
ROCK 'N' ROLL: Beautiful painted women
X ADVANTAGE: Rock

HOW THEY GET TO THE ARENA:
SPORTS: On a bus with the coach
ROCK 'N' ROLL: In a limo with Sweet Sweet Connie
X ADVANTAGE: Rock 'n' Roll

BEST MOVIES:
SPORTS: *Slap Shot*
ROCK 'N' ROLL: Still waiting...
X ADVANTAGE: Sports

MOMENTS THAT TRY MEN'S SOULS:
SPORTS: Settling for a field goal
ROCK 'N' ROLL: Staying conscious through the drum solo
X ADVANTAGE: Sports. At least you put some points on the board.

PLAYING HURT:
SPORTS: Calling audibles with a concussion
ROCK 'N' ROLL: Singing with a new tongue stud
– – ADVANTAGE: Push

FOREIGN SUBSTANCES:
SPORTS: On the ball
ROCK 'N' ROLL: In the bloodstream
X ADVANTAGE: Sports

UNSUNG FEMALE PIONEERS:
SPORTS: Manon Rheaume
ROCK 'N' ROLL: Suzi Quatro
X ADVANTAGE: Sports

SCAPEGOATS:
SPORTS: Buckner
ROCK 'N' ROLL: Yoko
– – ADVANTAGE: Push

RIVALRIES:
SPORTS: Bills-Dolphins
ROCK 'N' ROLL: Christina-Britney
X ADVANTAGE: Rock 'n' Roll—I loves me a catfight.

PEP SQUAD:
SPORTS: Morganna
ROCK 'N' ROLL: Pamela Des Barres
X ADVANTAGE: Rock 'n' Roll

WHAT FANS HURL:
SPORTS: Batteries
ROCK 'N' ROLL: Room keys
X ADVANTAGE: Rock 'n' Roll

OXYMORONS:
SPORTS: Utah Jazz
ROCK 'N' ROLL: KISS Unplugged
X ADVANTAGE: Sports

THEY REINVENTED THE NATIONAL ANTHEM:
SPORTS: Carl Lewis
ROCK 'N' ROLL: Jimi Hendrix
X ADVANTAGE: Rock 'n' Roll

UNFORGETTABLE TELEVISION MOMENTS:
ROCK 'N' ROLL: The Beatles on *Ed Sullivan*
SPORTS: Bobby Knight at a press conference
X ADVANTAGE: Rock 'n' Roll

YOU KNOW IT'S OVER WHEN:
SPORTS: You hold your fourth retirement press conference
ROCK 'N' ROLL: *Behind the Music* calls
X ADVANTAGE: Sports

HAIRSTYLES THAT NEVER CAUGHT ON:
SPORTS: The Don King
ROCK 'N' ROLL: A Flock of Seagulls
X ADVANTAGE: Sports

BEST BITES:
SPORTS: Mike Tyson vs. Holyfield
ROCK 'N' ROLL: Ozzy Osborne vs. Dove
X ADVANTAGE: Sports

So there you have it; it's so simple when you break things down scientifically. In the fight of the century, the advantage goes to sports. Where else can you watch a penalty shot and hear AC/DC blasting at the same time? Until next time, I'm Nick Bakay, reminding you the numbers never lie.

Bad Boys

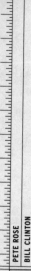

PETE ROSE
BILL CLINTON

What's more shocking—Bill Clinton getting eight figures to pen his memoir, or *Vanity Fair* bumping the requisite Donatella Versace article for one about Pete Rose? Oh, how the mighty have fallen, but which one fell hardest? The Pimp Daddy Prez versus Charlie Point Spread—we may never know the truth, but we sure as hell can set these two scandal-plagued he-men in the ring and see how they stack up at the Tale of the Tape...

WEAKNESSES:
ROSE: Teasers
CLINTON: Teases
ADVANTAGE: Push

INJURED PARTIES WAITING AT HOME:
ROSE: Ray Fosse
CLINTON: Hillary
ADVANTAGE: Rose

LEGENDS THEY ECLIPSED:
ROSE: Ty Cobb
CLINTON: JFK
ADVANTAGE: Push

HOT READING:
ROSE: When the *Dowd Report* uses words like "parlay"
CLINTON: Chapter twelve of his memoir, "Et Tu Chubby Chaser"
ADVANTAGE: Clinton

THE FATHER OF:
ROSE: The mullet
CLINTON: The first lubricant with the Presidential Seal
ADVANTAGE: Clinton

FAMOUS QUOTES IN THEIR ORIGINAL FORM:
ROSE: "I did not bet on baseball... that was my evil twin."
CLINTON: "I feel your pain... it's in your left breast."
ADVANTAGE: Clinton. *Meep-meep!*

WHERE THERE'S SMOKE, THERE'S... :
ROSE: One of Marge Schott's Tarreytons
CLINTON: A Cuban resting in the world's chubbiest humidor
ADVANTAGE: Push, and pass the barf bag.

THE MARKET PRICE FOR MEMORIES
ROSE: $500 per signed bat forged by Tom Gioiosa
CLINTON: $1,000,000 per peccadillo
ADVANTAGE: Clinton

AMAZING TALENTS:
ROSE: He needs only two syllables to say the name "Giamatti."
CLINTON: He's still married!
ADVANTAGE: Rose

NO PERSONAL CALLS:
ROSE: Using the dugout phone to call his bookie
CLINTON: Using that red phone for a booty call
ADVANTAGE: Push

WE FELT THEIR PAIN:
ROSE: When Jim Gray soiled the 50 Greatest Players ceremony
CLINTON: When we saw Paula Jones's pre-op pictures
ADVANTAGE: Push

WHERE YOU WON'T BE SEEING THEM SOON:
ROSE: The Hall of Fame
CLINTON: A Promise Keepers rally
ADVANTAGE: Clinton

So there you have it; it's all so simple when you break things down scientifically. In a photo finish with blackmail written all over it, the advantage... goes to an extremely rare push. One man has more base hits than anyone in the history of the game, while the other brought us a stock market that plumped our IRAs enough to forgive the scandals. I wish both were still playing. Until next time, I'm Nick Bakay, reminding you the numbers never lie.

LET'S RUN A SIMPLE CHECKLIST OF PROS AND CONS...

WHY/WHY NOT PETE SHOULD BE IN THE HALL

WHY: He has the most hits in baseball history.

WHY NOT: He once bet a C-note that Marge Schott knew all the lyrics to "Let's Get It On."

WHY: Charlie Hustle always played hard.

WHY NOT: The *Dowd Report* reads like a wiretap in the back room at Ba Da Bing!

WHY: He slid headfirst.

WHY NOT: He slid headfirst because he had a football teaser card in his back pocket.

WHY: The man has certainly paid his dues.

WHY NOT: Not quite sure he's paid the vig.

WHY: What an acceptance speech.

WHY NOT: And Jim Gray can't wait to ruin it.

WHY: Arguably the first mullet in baseball.

WHY NOT: First mullet in the hall.

As Pete continues to get passed over while the veterans' committee enshrines players named "Stumpy" Joe Magee, one thing is clear: A background check of many of Cooperstown's bronze plaques would read like "Caligula's West Coast Road Trip." Survey says let him in.

Bad Boys

Somewhere in the primordial bull pen of men's souls, we know: Once you go limp, the rest of the tribe will leave you behind with a few talismans, some jerky, and a new nickname—"Raptor Snack." Luckily for modern man, we've got the wonder drugs Viagra and steroids. Both have been discussed at owners' meetings. A lot. Now let's see how they stack up at the Tale of the Tape.

HOW TO SPOT A USER
STEROIDS: Sixty lbs. of new muscle in twenty-one days
VIAGRA: His wife is sorta quiet 'n' dreamy.
X ADVANTAGE: Viagra

ALCHEMY:
VIAGRA: Bananas into tungsten
STEROIDS: Plums into raisins
X ADVANTAGE: Viagra

SPOKESMAN:
STEROIDS: Mighty Joe Young
VIAGRA: Bob Dole—turned his pen into a Sharpie.
X ADVANTAGE: Viagra

INJECTIONS:
STEROIDS: Catching
VIAGRA: Pitching
X ADVANTAGE: Viagra

USER HANGOUTS:
STEROIDS: Gold's Gym
VIAGRA: The Senior Center Jacuzzi
X ADVANTAGE: Steroids

IMPROVES:
STEROIDS: Squats
VIAGRA: Thrusts
X ADVANTAGE: Viagra

SYNONYMOUS WITH:
STEROIDS: The NFL
VIAGRA: The Senior Tour
ADVANTAGE: Push X

ACCELERATES:
STEROIDS: Healing
VIAGRA: Booty calls
ADVANTAGE: Push X

USED BY CHINA'S FEMALE ATHLETES?:
STEROIDS: Yes
VIAGRA: Yes!
ADVANTAGE: Push

PROVIDERS:
VIAGRA: A doctor
STEROIDS: A former WWE star in a bandanna, hanging out near the deltoid machines
X ADVANTAGE: Viagra

EUPHEMISMS:
VIAGRA: Lead in your pencil
STEROIDS: Lead in your eyeballs
X ADVANTAGE: Viagra

RESULTS:
STEROIDS: A jawbone like Leno's
VIAGRA: A bulge like Diggler's
X ADVANTAGE: Viagra

DRAMATICALLY IMPROVES:
STEROIDS: Upper-body strength
VIAGRA: Vertical leap
ADVANTAGE: Push

DOWNSIDES:
STEROIDS: "Roid Rage"
VIAGRA: "Nasty Pants"
ADVANTAGE: Viagra

SIDE EFFECTS:
STEROIDS: Mood swings
VIAGRA: Child support
ADVANTAGE: Viagra

DO THEY PREVENT FATIGUE IN THE RED ZONE?:
STEROIDS: Yes
VIAGRA: Yes
ADVANTAGE: Push

USER NICKNAMES:
STEROIDS: Mankey
VIAGRA: Pantszilla
ADVANTAGE: Push

CLAIMS TO CREATE:
STEROIDS: Lean muscle mass
VIAGRA: Chubby muscle mass
ADVANTAGE: Push

POSSIBLE BRAND NAMES:
STEROIDS: "Throttle in a Bottle"
VIAGRA: "The High Hard One"
ADVANTAGE: Viagra

So there you have it; it's so simple when you break things down scientifically. In a final-lap *surge*, the advantage goes to Viagra! But have no fear, these are two performance enhancers that get you coming and going. And for God's sake, no one give this stuff to Shawn Kemp. Until next time, I'm Nick Bakay, reminding you the numbers never lie.

PLAY-OFF REFS
ROGUE COPS

They say power corrupts absolutely, but whatever beat he walks, when it comes to Johnny Law, inconsistency is a hard pill to swallow.

Looking for bad cops? The metro section of your local newspaper is riper than Nicaraguan street fruit. Obviously, a vast majority of cops are more than respectable, but the good ones just don't get the same pub.

Looking for bad officiating? Try the third period of an NHL play-off game, or, as I like to call it, "Mr. Whistle Takes a Holiday."

I say it's time to drop the puck and see who is the baddest of the bad lieutenants: play-off refs, rogue cops...let's see how they stack up at the Tale of the Tape...

INSPIRATIONS:
ROGUE COPS: Pirates
PLAY-OFF REFS: Rogue cops
X ADVANTAGE: Rogue cops

BENDING THE RULES:
ROGUE COPS: Pretty girls don't get speeding tickets.

PLAY-OFF REFS: Haven't called a third-period penalty since the Eisenhower administration.
- - ADVANTAGE: Push

SOUND BITES:
ROGUE COPS: "*What* pound of coke?!"
PLAY-OFF REFS: "He did *not*!!!"
- - ADVANTAGE: Push

QUALIFICATIONS:
ROGUE COPS: Nepotism
PLAY-OFF REFS: Thick ankles and thousands of pucks to the head
X ADVANTAGE: Rogue cops

EXISTING MEDICAL CONDITIONS:
ROGUE COPS: Sticky fingers
PLAY-OFF REFS: Selectively blurry vision, a.k.a. Mr. Magoo Syndrome
- - ADVANTAGE: Push

FREEBIES:
ROGUE COPS: Doughnuts
PLAY-OFF REFS: Trips to Ottawa
X ADVANTAGE: Rogue cops, with apologies to Don Koharski

OFT HEARD:
ROGUE COPS: "Step out of the vehicle, and leave the contraband inside."
PLAY-OFF REFS: "Don't make me warn you again, Mr. Domi."
- - ADVANTAGE: Push

HOTEL ALIASES:
ROGUE COPS: Sir Loots Alot
PLAY-OFF REFS: Big Chief Broken Whistle
X ADVANTAGE: Rogue cops

GETS THEIR PANTIES IN A BUNCH:
ROGUE COPS: A surprise visit from Internal Affairs
PLAY-OFF REFS: When the stadium organist plays "Three Blind Mice"
X ADVANTAGE: Refs

GOOD AT DODGING:
ROGUE COPS: Prosecution
PLAY-OFF REFS: Collisions
X | ADVANTAGE: Refs

WHERE THERE'S SMOKE:
PLAY-OFF REFS: Even the NHL won't let him work the play-offs, then revokes his Zamboni privileges.
ROGUE COPS: Drives to his fifth straight suspension hearing in a new Benz.
X | ADVANTAGE: Rogue cops

X-MAS BONUS:
ROGUE COPS: Thick envelopes from madams
PLAY-OFF REFS: A defenseman "accidentally" clears the puck through your 5-hole.
X | ADVANTAGE: Rogue cops

CAN'T A MAN RELAX?:
PLAY-OFF REFS: Summoning service at a strip club
ROGUE COPS: Serving summons at a strip club
– | – | ADVANTAGE: Push...

STRIPED SHIRTS:
ROGUE COPS: Dread 'em
PLAY-OFF REFS: Wear 'em
X | ADVANTAGE: Refs

BLADES:
ROGUE COPS: On their feet
PLAY-OFF REFS: Taped to their calves
– | – | ADVANTAGE: Push

ICING:
ROGUE COPS: Major penalty
PLAY-OFF REFS: Minor penalty
X | ADVANTAGE: Refs

IF THEY WERE SUPERHEROES:
ROGUE COPS: The power to plant evidence
PLAY-OFF REFS: The power to ignore blood on the ice
X | ADVANTAGE: Rogue cops. I love a gardener.

AVERAGE SALARY:
ROGUE COPS: $45,000...plus a house in Majorca
PLAY-OFF REFS: $175,000...plus all the hotel soap they can steal
– | – | ADVANTAGE: Push

WHERE THEY GO FROM HERE:
ROGUE COPS: Pro wrestling
PLAY-OFF REFS: Rogue cops
X | ADVANTAGE: Rogue cops

JUSTIFICATIONS:
ROGUE COPS: "Hey, my kids gotta eat!"
PLAY-OFF REFS: "Yes, Brett Hull was in the crease! Yes, we've called it all year, but it's getting late and the commissioner looks really tired!"
X | ADVANTAGE: Rogue cops

So there you have it; it's all so simple when you break things down scientifically. In a late whistle, the advantage... goes to play-off refs. But hang in there, Officer. If you're going to carry a grudge, remember—the whole rogue cop thing was my wife Robin's idea (Cal. license plate 3YOD224). Until next time, I'm Nick Bakay, reminding you the numbers never lie.

Bad Boys

PRICE
EUSTACHY

To quote Redd Foxx, "Can't a man *relax*?"

Apparently not.

Particularly if you're a college coach who leaves a stripper alone in his hotel room, or who parties with coeds on a rival campus after a loss. Just ask Larry "Nothing Good Happens After 4 A.M." Eustachy and Mike "Order Anything You Want" Price. I'm the last person to sit in moral judgment. Whatever did or didn't happen, I've done worse on a typical *Tuesday*. That being said, however, I'll never ask you to entrust me with your son for the next four to six years, depending on whether or not I want to red-shirt him. Eustachy and Price: Both are old enough to know that if you screw up in public, the wolves come out. So do the mean-spirited jokes. And away we go...

HOW YOU GET YOUR WIFE TO SIT BESIDE YOU AT THE PRESS CONFERENCE:

EUSTACHY: "You think there are no good shoe stores in *Iowa*? Try Appalachia! 'Cuz that's our next stop if we don't circle the wagons!"

PRICE: Slip a C-note in her support hose

ADVANTAGE: Push

FUTURE RECRUITING LINES:

EUSTACHY: "Have I told you about all the fantastic microbreweries in Iowa?"

PRICE: "Can a head coach get a table dance?!"

ADVANTAGE: Push

GENEROSITY:

EUSTACHY: Offered to buy the next twelve-pack

PRICE: Gave people a reason to forget Franchione's bailout

ADVANTAGE: Price

LESSONS LEARNED:

EUSTACHY: Never party with people too young to have ear hair.

PRICE: Never leave a stripper alone with your credit card and a hotel room service menu.

ADVANTAGE: Push

TURNING POINTS:
EUSTACHY: "You're *sure* that camera's not loaded?"
PRICE: "Anybody want to see if *The Hours* made it to my hotel Spectravision?"
ADVANTAGE: Push

PICKUP LINES:
EUSTACHY: "Isn't Missouri the Show Me State?"
PRICE: "Those are fake?! Let me get a closer look..."
ADVANTAGE: Push

HONORABLE MENTION:
EUSTACHY: "Who wants to pet the enemy?"
PRICE: "Destiny? Is that your *real* name?"
ADVANTAGE: Eustachy

WHAT REALLY COST HIM HIS JOB:
EUSTACHY: A losing record in his conference
PRICE: An AmEx bill
ADVANTAGE: Push

PROBABLY SHOULD HAVE:
EUSTACHY: Stayed in his room and emptied the minibar
PRICE: Actually signed that ten-million-dollar contract
ADVANTAGE: Push

THE NCAA'S TAKE:
EUSTACHY: "We still get all that tournament money, right?"
PRICE: "Hey, it's not like he paid for a kid to fly home for a funeral."
ADVANTAGE: Push

PERSONAL MOTTOES:
EUSTACHY: Keep your lips on a tall boy or a short girl.
PRICE: It ain't cheatin' if you're in Florida.
ADVANTAGE: Push

$1,000 IN HOTEL CHARGES?:
EUSTACHY: One bottle of Excedrin, and forty-eight local calls trying to piece together exactly what the hell you did last night
PRICE: That's a lot of Doritos stuffed in a G-string. Either she's trying to bulk up for the combines, or she worked up a nice appetite.
ADVANTAGE: Push

PRICELESS:
EUSTACHY: Video of him slurring through a karaoke performance of "The Gambler"
PRICE: Keeping the Membership Reward points
ADVANTAGE: Price

HOW THEY BROKE IT TO THEIR FAMILIES:
EUSTACHY: Funny story, heh heh...
PRICE: Funny story, heh heh...
ADVANTAGE: PUSH

So there you have it; it's all so simple when you break things down scientifically. In a tawdry collision of mid-to-late-life crises, the advantage goes to push. And I think we've all learned an important lesson: When it comes to survival in the spotlight of amateur athletics, you're far better off Bobby Knighting your players to bruise city than you are Eustachying a few beers and Pricing a lap dance. Until next time, I'm Nick Bakay, reminding you the numbers never lie.

LOCAL BOOKIE OFFSHORE

What's the point of watching a game when you can *bleed* over it? I'm talking action, my friends, the kind that adds life or death proportions to the score crawl on the bottom of your screen. The variable is where you place your bets—with the local guy, or the virtual Caribbean casino? Either way, you're sure to reduce your kid's college fund to an empty bucket of sweaty excuses and second mortgages, something I call *just livin' the dream!* But is it that simple? Let's see how they stack up at the Tale of the Tape…

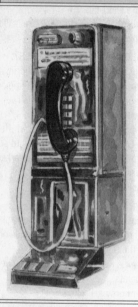

EXOTIC LOCATIONS:
LOCAL BOOKIE: The back booth at Bob's Classy Lady
OFFSHORE SPORTS BOOK: Costa Rica
X ADVANTAGE: Local!

DO THEY GIVE CREDIT?:
LOCAL BOOKIE: Yes
OFFSHORE SPORTS BOOK: No
X ADVANTAGE: Local bookie, until you're hiding from him in Mexico

HOW YOU MAKE CONTACT:
LOCAL BOOKIE: A grimy pay phone teeming with SARS
OFFSHORE SPORTS BOOK: One doomed click of the ol' mouse
X ADVANTAGE: Offshore

THINGS YOU DON'T WANT TO HEAR:
LOCAL BOOKIE: "Vic's dead, who may I say is calling?"
OFFSHORE SPORTS BOOK: "The Government of Antigua has collapsed!"
-- ADVANTAGE: Push

LEGALITIES:

LOCAL BOOKIE: The FBI has tapped his phones ever since the Colts lost to the Jets in '69.

OFFSHORE SPORTS BOOK: Turns out sportsandsexyladies.com was really a front for the Taliban.

ADVANTAGE: Push

WARDROBE:

LOCAL BOOKIE: Visor, armbands, shoulder holster

OFFSHORE SPORTS BOOK: Cutoff khakis with rope belt

ADVANTAGE: Local

RETRIBUTION:

LOCAL BOOKIE: Joey Bag O' Doughnuts introduces your kidneys to thirty-two ounces of Louisville Slugger.

OFFSHORE SPORTS BOOK: Explaining to your wife why her Mercedes is now a Razor scooter.

ADVANTAGE: Offshore—I mean, she still loves you, right?...Hellooo?

BAD IMPULSES:

LOCAL BOOKIE: You let it ride on the Clippers.

OFFSHORE SPORTS BOOK: You blow your teaser profits in the convenient virtual Pai Gow room.

ADVANTAGE: Push

YOUR WORST FEAR:

LOCAL BOOKIE: His real last name is Gotti.

OFFSHORE SPORTS BOOK: Your "account rep" is actually a nineteen-year-old with a taste for crystal meth.

ADVANTAGE: Push

PAYOUTS:

LOCAL BOOKIE: Sure, if you're willing to accept a greasy brown paper bag at an all-night doughnut shop.

OFFSHORE SPORTS BOOK: Maybe

ADVANTAGE: Local. I hear the post office is training parlay-sniffing dogs.

PROBLEMS FILING A COMPLAINT:

LOCAL BOOKIE: He don't hear so good in the ear that got cut off.

OFFSHORE SPORTS BOOK: Ginger and Mary Ann refuse to put your desperate call through to Gilligan.

ADVANTAGE: Push

HIDDEN TALENTS:

LOCAL BOOKIE: Can recite the current line for twelve different sports.

OFFSHORE SPORTS BOOK: Can hike up a coconut tree in 4.5 seconds.

ADVANTAGE: Local

LATE PAYMENT PENALTIES:

LOCAL BOOKIE: He sold your kid on the black market.

OFFSHORE SPORTS BOOK: He hacked into your Visa account.

ADVANTAGE: Offshore

BAT SH:**

LOCAL BOOKIE: What he goes when you're late paying

OFFSHORE SPORTS BOOK: What he pays the locals in

ADVANTAGE: Offshore

THE VIG:

LOCAL BOOKIE: 2 percent, compounded hourly

OFFSHORE SPORTS BOOK: More Spam than the U.S. Army

ADVANTAGE: Push

HOW YOU MET:

LOCAL BOOKIE: Through your degenerate brother-in-law

OFFSHORE SPORTS BOOK: Through a link on beaversluts.com

ADVANTAGE: Push—the only winner here is depravity.

WHY YOU DO IT:

LOCAL BOOKIE: It adds excitement to your suburban ennui.

OFFSHORE SPORTS BOOK: They gave you $200 to get started.

ADVANTAGE: Local—that $200 will be gone faster than you can say over/under.

CODE WORDS:

LOCAL BOOKIE: "I'd like two packs of Juicy Fruit on the Panthers."

OFFSHORE SPORTS BOOK: Secret password: "Doodie head"

ADVANTAGE: Offshore

HOW YOU SNEAK AWAY FROM YOUR WIFE TO PLACE BETS:

LOCAL BOOKIE: "I'm gonna go pick up a pizza."

OFFSHORE SPORTS BOOK: "I'm gonna go Google puppies..."

ADVANTAGE: Push

UNDERRATED SIDE EFFECTS:

LOCAL BOOKIE: You now know your way around the skanky part of town.

OFFSHORE SPORTS BOOK: You've found the only thing that can make the woman in your life yearn for the days when you spent six hours a night surfing porn.

ADVANTAGE: Local—skanky has its virtues.

So there you have it; it's all so simple when you break things down scientifically. In a one-way ticket to the flophouse, the advantage goes to push—either way, you lose the vig. But hang in there. I'm sure you've got a stone-cold lock that'll get you healthy in a hurry. Until next time, I'm Nick Bakay, reminding you the numbers never lie...

There's no joy in Mudville when baseball players go on strike. Of course, even at the minimum veteran salary, Mudville is a secluded millionaire enclave with an ocean view. Across town in the mansion on the hill, owners whine about losing money, and sell two years later with vigorish a Corleone would envy. Result? The cancellation of the 1994 World Series, and a close call with the only thing worse than no baseball: ownership's threat to field scab teams. Big Leaguers, No Leaguers. Let's see how they stack up at the Tale of the Tape...

PERSONNEL:
MAJOR LEAGUE BASEBALL: The best players in the world
SCAB BASEBALL: The best players who sobered up last Tuesday
X ADVANTAGE: Major League Baseball

TYPICAL PLAYER RÉSUMÉS:
MAJOR LEAGUE BASEBALL: Led majors in slugging percentage
SCAB BASEBALL: Drove a Coors truck
X ADVANTAGE: Major League Baseball

DEFINING QUALITIES:
MAJOR LEAGUE BASEBALL: Arrogance
SCAB BASEBALL: Desperation
-- ADVANTAGE: Push

SHORTSTOPS:
MAJOR LEAGUE BASEBALL: Goes to his right well
SCAB BASEBALL: Goes to his right well for a guy who breaks a sweat tying his shoes
X ADVANTAGE: Major League Baseball

TYPICAL PLAYER COMPLAINTS:
MAJOR LEAGUE BASEBALL: "I hate playing a day game after a night game."
SCAB BASEBALL: "Quit throwin' so hard; my hand's killin' me!"
-- ADVANTAGE: Push...no winners here.

ATTENDANCE:
MAJOR LEAGUE BASEBALL: 50–60 million league wide
SCAB BASEBALL: A Brooklyn Bridge jumper gets a better crowd.
X ADVANTAGE: Major League Baseball

SURPRISING TALENT POOLS:
MAJOR LEAGUE BASEBALL: San Pedro de Macoris, the Island of Shortstops
SCAB BASEBALL: The Rascal House Pub, the cul-de-sac of half-decent American Legion players
X ADVANTAGE: Major League Baseball

UNIFORMS:
MAJOR LEAGUE BASEBALL: Pinstripes
SCAB BASEBALL: Thongs!
X ADVANTAGE: Scab baseball, and a little something for the ladies!

ANTHEM:
MAJOR LEAGUE BASEBALL: "The Star-Spangled Banner"
SCAB BASEBALL: "Slow Ride," Foghat
-- ADVANTAGE: Push

TRADITIONS:
MAJOR LEAGUE BASEBALL: The seventh-inning stretch
SCAB BASEBALL: The fourth-inning conga line to the parking lot
X ADVANTAGE: Major League Baseball

MEMORIES ARE MADE OF THESE:
MAJOR LEAGUE BASEBALL: A twi-night doubleheader, just me and Dad
SCAB BASEBALL: A twi-night doubleheader, just me, my "new" dad, and his acne-pitted "first" son
X ADVANTAGE: Major League Baseball

So there you have it; it's all so simple when you break things down scientifically. This time, the advantage goes to...football! If you still feel a deep-seated need to care, maybe it's time to pour your heart into the sport with the healthiest collective bargaining agreement. Until next time, I'm Nick Bakay, reminding you the numbers never lie.

UMPS VS. AIR TRAFFIC CONTROLLERS

I don't care whether you wear your chest protector outside or under a jacket, umpire is a job that comes with No Love. Even your mother's going to bag on you and ask why you didn't consider a career in phone sales. Now, balance that malaise against the umpire union's recent negotiations, and you are looking at the most doomed walkout since Ronald Reagan imperiled every traveling American by crushing the air traffic controllers. Umpires, air traffic controllers, let's see how they stack up at the Tale of the Tape...

FLAWED STRIKE LOGIC:

UMPIRES: "Let's see, the fans hate us, the players hate us, the owners hate us...let's issue an ultimatum!"

AIR TRAFFIC CONTROLLERS: "Hey, it's not like they can fire us..."

ADVANTAGE: Push. There are no winners here.

BODY TYPES:

AIR TRAFFIC CONTROLLERS: Wiry and nervous

UMPIRES: Somewhere between porcine and reclining sea lion

ADVANTAGE: Air traffic controllers

SCAB EUPHEMISMS:

AIR TRAFFIC CONTROLLERS: Tower monkeys, blip jockeys, radar rooters

UMPIRES: Scumps

ADVANTAGE: Scumps

ON-THE-JOB HAZARDS:

UMPIRES: A foul tip off the facemask

AIR TRAFFIC CONTROLLERS: A wing tip off the tower!

ADVANTAGE: Umps

FITTED FOR:

UMPIRES: A girdle before your annual physical

AIR TRAFFIC CONTROLLERS: A catheter for a busy Sunday night

ADVANTAGE: Push

AT STAKE:
AIR TRAFFIC CONTROLLERS: Lives
UMPIRES: Billions of illegally wagered dollars
ADVANTAGE: Umps `X`

ONLY FOURTEEN MINUTES LONG:
AIR TRAFFIC CONTROLLERS: A typical shift
UMPIRES: A typical third strike call
ADVANTAGE: Air traffic controllers—there's no taunting in baseball! `X`

STRIKE ZONE:
UMPIRES: Anything between my third chin and that little pouchy underbelly that's sprouting in the shade of my gelatinous gut
AIR TRAFFIC CONTROLLERS: Anything between the buildings and the water
ADVANTAGE: Push `- -`

GUILTY CONFESSIONS:
UMPIRES: "My own stomach obstructed my view!"
AIR TRAFFIC CONTROLLERS: "Wuh-oh...Hey, anybody seen that FedEx plane?"
ADVANTAGE: Umps `X`

HARANGUED BY:
UMPIRES: Managers
AIR TRAFFIC CONTROLLERS: Survivors
ADVANTAGE: Air traffic controllers `X`

HOW THEY PAY THEIR DUES:
UMPIRES: Ten years in the minors
AIR TRAFFIC CONTROLLERS: Announcing demolition derbies
ADVANTAGE: Umps `X`

ODD BEHAVIOR AT HOME:
UMPIRES: When he whisk-brushes the dinner plate
AIR TRAFFIC CONTROLLERS: When he uses two flashlights to signal his daughter up to the garage
ADVANTAGE: Air traffic controllers `X`

WAYS TO UNWIND:
AIR TRAFFIC CONTROLLERS: Most airports are near the strip clubs.
UMPIRES: Don't have to leave the premises to drink.
ADVANTAGE: Air traffic controllers `X`

SCOURGES:
UMPIRES: Instant replay
AIR TRAFFIC CONTROLLERS: The black box
- - ADVANTAGE: Push

GUILTY PLEASURES:
UMPIRES: Calling a third strike on Roberto Alomar before the ball is even pitched
AIR TRAFFIC CONTROLLERS: The relaxing video of fish that runs during pre-boarding
X ADVANTAGE: Umps

CROWD CHANTS:
UMPIRES: The ump forgot his lunch. Eat it, ump! Eat it!
AIR TRAFFIC CONTROLLERS: Ladies and gentlemen, we're out of the chicken.
- - ADVANTAGE: Push

WORST FEARS:
UMPIRES: Ending the World Series on a blown call
AIR TRAFFIC CONTROLLERS: Landing a plane before the movie's over
X ADVANTAGE: Umps

UNDESIRABLE NICKNAMES:
UMPIRES: Ol' Strikes for Balls
AIR TRAFFIC CONTROLLERS: Ol' Foam on the Runway
X ADVANTAGE: Umps

A LAYOVER IN PITTSBURGH:
AIR TRAFFIC CONTROLLERS: An unfortunate mistake

UMPIRES: One last chance to pig out at Sbarro before the wife puts you on that diet
X ADVANTAGE: Air traffic controllers

SCUFFED BALLS:
UMPIRES: Something to watch out for
AIR TRAFFIC CONTROLLERS: Something to hope for
X ADVANTAGE: Air traffic controllers

SECRET DESIRES:
AIR TRAFFIC CONTROLLERS: To join the Mile High Club
UMPIRES: To see their toes while standing
X ADVANTAGE: Air traffic controllers

NO-NOS:
UMPIRES: Whispering sweet nothings as you crouch behind the catcher's ear
AIR TRAFFIC CONTROLLERS: Playing Tetris while landing a 747
X ADVANTAGE: Umps

FIGHTING BACK!:
UMPIRES: Bumping players!
AIR TRAFFIC CONTROLLERS: Making arrogant pilots say your name before landing
X ADVANTAGE: Air traffic controllers

WHO CARES?:
AIR TRAFFIC CONTROLLERS: Everyone who is cleared for landing
UMPIRES: Everyone with money on the game!
- - ADVANTAGE: Push!

So there you have it; it's so simple when you break things down scientifically. In a devastating blow to union solidarity, the advantage goes to air traffic controllers. Hey, I'm from Buffalo—you didn't really think I was going to side with any officiating after Brett Hull was in the crease, did you? Until next time, I'm Nick Bakay, reminding you the numbers never lie.

ULTIMATE FIGHTING / BUM FIGHTS

Ultimate Fighting filled an audience void by coming on like boxing's unstable half brother. Then we found a way to take it down a couple, three hundred, notches with Bum Fights—and I don't mean the ones that take place at English boarding schools. I'm talking weaselly film school grads videotaping flophouse fights that come on like Ultimate Fighting's degenerate uncle Chappy. Both have been banned in many states, yet both have uncovered a vital market for gruesome beatings filed under the heading "Things I Can't Un-See." Ultimate Fighting yearns for respectability, Bum Fights thrive on complete depravity, both are just begging to be stacked up at the Tale of the Tape, and may God have mercy on all of us…

ABSOLUTE CONFIRMATION:
ULTIMATE FIGHTING: That bouncers can advance in this world
BUM FIGHTS: That some people will do anything for a pint of Wild Irish Rose
ADVANTAGE: Push

PATRON SAINTS:
ULTIMATE FIGHTING: Mitch "Blood" Green
BUM FIGHTS: Charles Bukowski
ADVANTAGE: Bum Fights

TYPICAL FIGHTER NICKNAMES:
ULTIMATE FIGHTING: Dan "The Hell Bat" Turner
BUM FIGHTS: John Doe
ADVANTAGE: Bum fights. It doesn't tip the outcome.

VIRTUES:
ULTIMATE FIGHTING: Don King hasn't found a way to cheapen it…yet.
BUM FIGHTS: It's a nice way to sober up from a three-day bender.
ADVANTAGE: Bum Fights

TECHNIQUES:
ULTIMATE FIGHTING: Brazilian Jiu Jitsu
BUM FIGHTS: The Ol' Puke and Juke
ADVANTAGE: Push

ARENAS:
ULTIMATE FIGHTING: The Octagon
BUM FIGHTS: The Alley Behind the Blood Bank
ADVANTAGE: Bum Fights

YOU COULD BE DISQUALIFIED FOR:
ULTIMATE FIGHTING: Nothing
BUM FIGHTS: Fighting imaginary insects
ADVANTAGE: Ultimate Fighting

COMBATANTS HAVE ENTERED:
ULTIMATE FIGHTING: A world of hurt
BUM FIGHTS: Bottoming-out's basement
ADVANTAGE: Push

PROMOTIONAL BODY MARKINGS:
ULTIMATE FIGHTING: Goldenpalace.com
BUM FIGHTS: Just Say No to Rehab
ADVANTAGE: Bum Fights

TALENT-RICH HOT SPOTS:
ULTIMATE FIGHTING: Dojos in a bad part of town
BUM FIGHTS: Empty refrigerator boxes in a good part of town
ADVANTAGE: Ultimate Fighting

ULTIMATE FIGHTING VS. BUM FIGHTS

PLAY-BY-PLAY HIGHLIGHTS:
ULTIMATE FIGHTING: "Ooh, both fighters have their heads between each other's thighs..."
BUM FIGHTS: "He's got the trash can lid...Oh, crap, let's get out of here!"
ADVANTAGE: Push

SOMETIMES IT'S HARD TO TELL:
ULTIMATE FIGHTING: When to stop the fight
BUM FIGHTS: When the fight has started
ADVANTAGE: Ultimate Fighting

PROUD SPONSORS:
ULTIMATE FIGHTING: Stypticpencil.com
BUM FIGHTS: Republican tax cuts
ADVANTAGE: Ultimate Fighting

PROOF POSITIVE:
ULTIMATE FIGHTING: People will wait in line to watch a good beating
BUM FIGHTS: The death of empathy
ADVANTAGE: Push

Nick Bakay's Tale of the Tape

PURSE:
ULTIMATE FIGHTING: Six figures
BUM FIGHTS: A beer buzz and an egg sandwich
ADVANTAGE: Push—by the time everyone gets their cut, you're looking at a beer buzz and an egg sandwich.

SEEING DOUBLE:
ULTIMATE FIGHTING: After
BUM FIGHTS: What did you two say?
ADVANTAGE: Push

IMPOSSIBLE TO DEFEND AGAINST:
ULTIMATE FIGHTING: A low, crab style
BUM FIGHTS: The squirts
ADVANTAGE: Ultimate Fighting

DELIVERY SYSTEMS:
ULTIMATE FIGHTING: Pay Per View
BUM FIGHTS: A trembling camcorder
ADVANTAGE: Ultimate Fighting

A FRONT-ROW SEAT MEANS:
ULTIMATE FIGHTING: More spray than a Gallagher concert
BUM FIGHTS: Inevitable crab infestation
ADVANTAGE: Push

WHERE THE RAGE COMES FROM:
ULTIMATE FIGHTING: Bad Daddy
BUM FIGHTS: "Who stole my shoes?!"
ADVANTAGE: Push

UNFORTUNATE SIDE EFFECTS:
ULTIMATE FIGHTING: Pugilistic dementia
BUM FIGHTS: Good old-fashioned schizophrenia
ADVANTAGE: Push

WAGERING:
ULTIMATE FIGHTING: Vegas odds, Vegas action
BUM FIGHTS: "I got two bucks on the guy with the tin-foil helmet!"
ADVANTAGE: Push—action is action.

UNBELIEVABLE:
ULTIMATE FIGHTING: How they get up and walk when it's over
BUM FIGHTS: How many of them have "III" after the X they sign on the release form
ADVANTAGE: Bum Fights

SECOND CHANCES:
ULTIMATE FIGHTING: To get even with everyone who called him pencil dick
BUM FIGHTS: For his relatives to finally locate him
ADVANTAGE: Bum Fights

AFTER-PARTIES:
ULTIMATE FIGHTING: The coolest club in town
BUM FIGHTS: Twenty minutes in the director's heated van
ADVANTAGE: Ultimate Fighting

So there you have it; it's all so simple when you break things down scientifically. In a gestating subdural hematoma, the advantage goes to...exploitation. On the plus side, it probably won't be long before we see "The World's Bloodiest Baby Brawls." Until next time, I'm Nick Bakay, reminding you the numbers never lie.

Bad Boys

Is it just me, or are good and evil relative terms? Regardless, struggling with them may be part of the human experience, but that's not to stop us from breaking them down and seeing how they stack up at the Tale of the Tape.

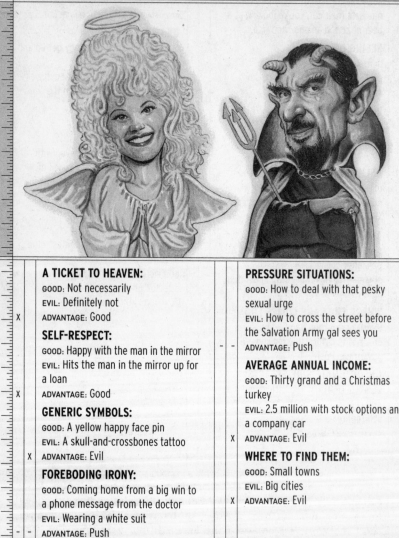

A TICKET TO HEAVEN:
GOOD: Not necessarily
EVIL: Definitely not

[X] ADVANTAGE: Good

SELF-RESPECT:
GOOD: Happy with the man in the mirror
EVIL: Hits the man in the mirror up for a loan

[X] ADVANTAGE: Good

GENERIC SYMBOLS:
GOOD: A yellow happy face pin
EVIL: A skull-and-crossbones tattoo

[X] ADVANTAGE: Evil

FOREBODING IRONY:
GOOD: Coming home from a big win to a phone message from the doctor
EVIL: Wearing a white suit

[- -] ADVANTAGE: Push

PRESSURE SITUATIONS:
GOOD: How to deal with that pesky sexual urge
EVIL: How to cross the street before the Salvation Army gal sees you

[- -] ADVANTAGE: Push

AVERAGE ANNUAL INCOME:
GOOD: Thirty grand and a Christmas turkey
EVIL: 2.5 million with stock options and a company car

[X] ADVANTAGE: Evil

WHERE TO FIND THEM:
GOOD: Small towns
EVIL: Big cities

[X] ADVANTAGE: Evil

PREFERRED CARS:
GOOD: Six-cylinder, fuel-efficient SUVs to haul around the kids
EVIL: Eight-cylinder, high-performance vehicles with large trunks, radar detectors, and an e-ject-o seat
X ADVANTAGE: Evil

ADEPT AT DOWNLOADING MP3S:
GOOD: No
EVIL: No
– – ADVANTAGE: Push—no winners here.

UNUSUAL SKILLS:
GOOD: The ability to survive parenthood
EVIL: The ability to dig one's way out of a cell with a toothbrush
X ADVANTAGE: Good, in a squeaker

HUMBLE THOUGHTS:
GOOD: Honor those who died for America.
EVIL: Screw the dead. Let's kill the rest with cyanide-laced headache relief medication.
X ADVANTAGE: Good

LURKS IN THEIR HEARTS:
GOOD: Do the right thing.
EVIL: Do the right thing to reap personal dividends.
X ADVANTAGE: Good

DISCIPLINE:
GOOD: Gives his kid a time out and a stern talking-to.
EVIL: Gives his kid a Milk-Bone and a night in the backyard doghouse.
X ADVANTAGE: Evil. A place of your own is a place of your own.

FEED THE WORLD:
GOOD: Makes a tidy profit exporting agricultural products to other countries
EVIL: Classifies cigarettes as an agricultural product
– – ADVANTAGE: Push

SOMETHING THEY WOULD LIKE TO CHANGE:
GOOD: Increase tolerance and lower taxes
EVIL: Increase loopholes and lower standards
X ADVANTAGE: Good

MECCAS:
GOOD: Churches and malls
EVIL: Churches and Swiss banks
– – ADVANTAGE: Evil

WHAT THEY DO IN LAS VEGAS:
GOOD: Ooh and aah over at the theme hotels
EVIL: Ooh and aah over the vig
– – ADVANTAGE: Push

FAVORITE THING ABOUT *SPORTS-CENTER*:
GOOD: The sports coverage
EVIL: Nick Bakay
X ADVANTAGE: Evil

So there you have it; it's so simple when you break things down scientifically. In a just-this-once-and-I'll-never-do-it-again sign of Armageddon, the advantage goes to—uh-oh, the advantage goes to evil! I'm at a loss here, folks. Until next time, I'm Nick Bakay, slinking out the back door and reminding you that the numbers never lie. But evil usually does...

Bad Boys

Girls Girls Girls

FRENCH OPEN WITH ANNA KOURNIKOVA VS. WITHOUT HER

I think I speak for thinking and feeling men everywhere when I say it's time for Anna Kournikova to be better! But until that fine day, a sad tradition continues: Men eagerly usher their wives off to the mall, then hunker down for a lusty afternoon of women's tennis, only to see the best thing that has happened to the game since visible panties...get eliminated. Now what? Channel-hop over to Showtime in the hopes of catching a women's prison movie? The odds are you'll be stuck with a free afternoon and nothing worthy of filling the hole in your heart left by a naughty girl with a case of the first-round yips. You can't even say, "We still have Paris."

So it's time to sift through the carnage of what might have been: The French Open *with* Anna versus the French Open *without* her—let's see how they stack up at the Tale of the Tape...

POUTY:
WITHOUT ANNA: You
WITH ANNA: Her
ADVANTAGE: With

AUDIENCE DEMOGRAPHICS:
WITHOUT ANNA: A smattering of country clubbers
WITH ANNA: Every American male who doesn't suffer from glaucoma
ADVANTAGE: With

IF YOU LISTEN CLOSELY, YOU CAN HEAR VIEWERS MUTTER:
WITHOUT ANNA: "What, now I have to learn the rules of the game?"
WITH ANNA: "Who's your daddy?"
ADVANTAGE: Push

WHAT IT'S ALL ABOUT:
WITHOUT ANNA: Tennis
WITH ANNA: Balls
ADVANTAGE: With

Nick Bakay's Tale of the Tape

SURRENDER:

WITHOUT ANNA: You have no reason not to accompany your wife to see *The Vagina Monologues*. Again.

WITH ANNA: You have a new appreciation for the concept of mixed doubles.

X ADVANTAGE: With

SAY IT AIN'T SO:

WITHOUT ANNA: The other players are relieved as the focus shifts back to the game.

WITH ANNA: The tour prohibits bare midriffs.

X ADVANTAGE: Without, in a shocker!

THE RISKS YOU TAKE:

WITHOUT ANNA: You find yourself napping at 10 A.M.

WITH ANNA: Your wife comes home early and catches you practicing your forehand.

– – ADVANTAGE: Push

ACTION IN THE STANDS:

WITHOUT ANNA: Andre and Steffi making out

WITH ANNA: Fights break out between every Russian who has ever played in the NHL.

X ADVANTAGE: With

LOVE:

WITHOUT ANNA: A tie score

WITH ANNA: That crazy thing you're in

X ADVANTAGE: With

TOWELING OFF:

WITHOUT ANNA: Them

WITH ANNA: You, and your Barcalounger

ADVANTAGE: Push

FOOT FAULT:

WITHOUT ANNA: Loss of serve

WITH ANNA: Why can't she play in heels?

ADVANTAGE: Push

MUSINGS:

WITHOUT ANNA: Maybe she's using the free time to shoot a calendar...a nude calendar...at my house.

WITH ANNA: Maybe they'll run that commercial where she gives those dudes a BMW.

ADVANTAGE: Push

TRASH TALK:

WITHOUT ANNA: Hearing yourself call the gal who eliminated her "a minion of Satan"

WITH ANNA: Hearing her call her opponent a cow in broken English

X ADVANTAGE: With

NET BALL:

WITHOUT ANNA: A lame first serve

WITH ANNA: A chance that she might bend over and pick it up

X ADVANTAGE: With

THOUGHTS SCRIBBLED ON A NAPKIN:

WITHOUT ANNA: "Note to self: Stab eyes out."

WITH ANNA: "Mr. Anna Kournikova..."

– – ADVANTAGE: Push—nobody wins with random doodles, kids.

So there you have it; it's so simple when you break things down scientifically. In the hair-pulling catfight of your dreams, the advantage...goes to the French Open with Anna, but then again, twelve network executives and a monkey could have told you that. Until next time, I'm Nick Bakay, reminding you the numbers never lie.

DOMINATOR VS. DOMINATRIX

For some, relaxation means popping a cold pilsner and hunkering down with some play-off hockey. For others, it might involve a latex mask, a dungeon, and the hot sting of a hairbrush.

I don't judge.

But it's my job to get to the bottom of things and sort out who's the top, and who's the bottom. And in a world that includes a cruel and merciless goalie like Dominik Hasek, who better to face off with the Dominator than the unstoppable force of the pain and leisure industry...the Dominatrix. The fact is, you don't score on either, but who truly dominates? Let's see how they stack up at the Tale of the Tape...

SABRE:
DOMINATOR: His former team
DOMINATRIX: $50 extra
ADVANTAGE: Hasek

THE THIN RED LINE:
DOMINATOR: Separates a save from a goal
DOMINATRIX: Separates pleasure from pain
ADVANTAGE: Push

SIGNATURE MOVES:
DOMINATOR: A sprawling, snow angel save
DOMINATRIX: The gentle pop at the end of a whip
ADVANTAGE: Hasek

VULCANIZED RUBBER:
DOMINATOR: Pucks
DOMINATRIX: Pants
ADVANTAGE: Dominatrix

THE FIVE HOLE:
DOMINATOR: The space between his leg pads
DOMINATRIX: The new space she just added to your rib cage
ADVANTAGE: Push

TOP SHELF, WHERE MOMMA HIDES THE COOKIES:
DOMINATOR: The best place to score on him
DOMINATRIX: A role-playing game
ADVANTAGE: Push

HIDDEN DAINTIES:
DOMINATOR: Garter and hose
DOMINATRIX: Clamps and rings
X ADVANTAGE: Hasek

RED LIGHT:
DOMINATOR: A sure sign he let in a goal
DOMINATRIX: A sure sign you're in her neighborhood
X ADVANTAGE: Dominatrix

PENALTIES:
DOMINATOR: Two minutes in the sin-bin
DOMINATRIX: Two minutes out of it
X ADVANTAGE: Hasek

FANS WEAR:
DOMINATOR: Hasek jerseys
DOMINATRIX: Dog collars
X ADVANTAGE: Hasek

PLAYING HURT:
DOMINATOR: A nuisance
DOMINATRIX: The whole point
X ADVANTAGE: Dominatrix

CREASE:
DOMINATOR: Polices 'em
DOMINATRIX: Makes 'em
ADVANTAGE: Push

YOU NEVER KNOW WHEN THEY'RE GOING TO:
DOMINATOR: Retire
DOMINATRIX: Lift your head out of the toilet
ADVANTAGE: Push

GOES DOWN EASILY:
DOMINATOR: Yes
DOMINATRIX: No
ADVANTAGE: Push

"SCREEN!":
DOMINATOR: What he yells when his vision is blocked
DOMINATRIX: The safe word you yell when you want her to stop
ADVANTAGE: Push

WHAT THEY LIVE FOR:
DOMINATOR: A shutout
DOMINATRIX: One pendulous, salty tear
ADVANTAGE: Push

A PRODUCT OF:
DOMINATOR: Czechoslovakia
DOMINATRIX: A bad childhood
X ADVANTAGE: Hasek

HOW THEY WOULD SPEND THEIR DAY WITH LORD STANLEY'S CUP:
DOMINATOR: Sit and gaze at it with family and friends
DOMINATRIX: Use it to break your fingers
X ADVANTAGE: Hasek

So there you have it; it's all so simple when you break things down scientifically. After a particularly rough and randy session, the advantage goes...to Dominik Hasek. You didn't really think the finest goaltender in the world was going to yield to anyone you can find in the Yellow Pages, did you? But hang in there, Trixy, I'm sure your loss will be your 4:00 appointment's gain. Until next time, I'm Nick Bakay, reminding you the numbers never lie.

SHOWBIZ PRIMA DONNAS
SPORTS PRIMA DONNAS

A box office giant refuses to come out of his trailer until someone agrees to detail his navel with a solid-gold Q-Tip.

A gridiron legend removes his helmet in the end zone so the whole world can revel in the superfreaky wonder that is *him*.

Prima donnas don't just happen, they are born of the wreckage when talent collides with ego. The entertainment world's always had 'em, but the world of sports is closing the gap. Which one earns bragging rights as the bottomless cup o' narcissistic need? Sports prima donnas versus showbiz prima donnas—let's see how they stack up at the Tale of the Tape...

A.K.A.S:

SHOWBIZ PRIMA DONNAS: Divas

SPORTS PRIMA DONNAS: Hotdogs

ADVANTAGE: Push. Both remain massively popular with the trend-setting gay community.

EARLY INDICATIONS:

SHOWBIZ PRIMA DONNAS: At birth, they tried to kill their siblings.

SPORTS PRIMA DONNAS: At birth, they spiked their own umbilical cords.

ADVANTAGE: Sports

LIFE EXPECTANCY:

SHOWBIZ PRIMA DONNAS: Five to ten years, then a sad comeback after rehab

SPORTS PRIMA DONNAS: Five to ten years, and then a sad comeback in the WWE

ADVANTAGE: Push

WORST FEARS:

SHOWBIZ PRIMA DONNAS: Their obituary will be bumped off the front page by a world tragedy.

SPORTS PRIMA DONNAS: Me and my mom won't make the cut for the next Campbell's Chunky Soup endorsement.

ADVANTAGE: Push—way to go, Mom.

TURN-ONS:

SHOWBIZ PRIMA DONNAS: Their own reflections in the shallow end of a Bel Air pool

SPORTS PRIMA DONNAS: Slow, kiss-my-ass home run trots

X ADVANTAGE: Sports. I'd like to see Liz Taylor yank one into the mezzanine.

TURN-OFFS:

SHOWBIZ PRIMA DONNAS: You, or anything to do with you

SPORTS PRIMA DONNAS: The whole "team concept" thing

- - ADVANTAGE: Push

MOTTOES:

SHOWBIZ PRIMA DONNAS: "...but enough about me. What did *you* think of my performance?"

SPORTS PRIMA DONNAS: "I'm a star, he's a flashlight, with better stats this year."

- - ADVANTAGE: Push

WHEN GOOD INTENTIONS GO BAD:

SHOWBIZ PRIMA DONNAS: Sending their stand-ins to visit sick kids

SPORTS PRIMA DONNAS: Visiting sick kids and insisting on autographing their X rays

- - ADVANTAGE: Push

NEGOTIATIONS:

SHOWBIZ PRIMA DONNAS: A weight clause guaranteeing all costars stay ten pounds heavier than them

SPORTS PRIMA DONNAS: Having the ghostwriter of their "autobiographies" killed

- - ADVANTAGE: Push

REACHING NEW LOWS:

SHOWBIZ PRIMA DONNAS: Going to a funeral for the photo op

SPORTS PRIMA DONNAS: Naming all five kids "George Foreman"

- - ADVANTAGE: PUSH

ENTOURAGE:

SHOWBIZ PRIMA DONNAS: Agent, manager, accountant, airbrush artist, cosmetic surgeon, astrologer

SPORTS PRIMA DONNAS: Hair-braider, tat-man, brander, homies, preacher, bodyguard

X ADVANTAGE: Sports. Face it—it's a fun list.

SPENDING HABITS:

SHOWBIZ PRIMA DONNAS: Planet Hollywood shares collapse, forcing sale of Humvee

SPORTS PRIMA DONNAS: Spend entire signing bonus at a shoe store, and miss fourteen child support payments

X ADVANTAGE: Showbiz

KEEPING THE DREAM ALIVE:

SHOWBIZ PRIMA DONNAS: Tucks 'n' sucks

SPORTS PRIMA DONNAS: Expansion

- - ADVANTAGE: Push

VANITY PROJECTS:

SHOWBIZ PRIMA DONNAS: Take B.P. with the Dodgers

SPORTS PRIMA DONNAS: Devote more time to their music career

- - ADVANTAGE: Push—no winners here

So there you have it; in a stunner sure to make it into *The National Enquirer*, the advantage goes to...push. Nobody wins with egos this big, unless you get paid well to polish them. Until next time, I'm Nick Bakay, reminding you the numbers never lie.

MEN'S HOOPS / WOMEN'S HOOPS

Basketball—the only team sport that boasts a degree of equality between the sexes. Bottom line, you can bet 'em both, college and pro...although my hat's off to anyone who knows his way around a WNBA teaser card.

However, with equality comes competition. As a man, I feel a deep-seated need to pick a clear winner. I don't care if it's on the playing field, in the boardroom, or on a romantic getaway, I want to see someone on top...It's time to examine the battle of the sexes: Men's hoops versus women's hoops—let's see how they stack up at the Tale of the Tape...

3 POINTS:
MEN'S HOOPS: A shot from way downtown
WOMEN'S HOOPS: "You're lazy, your promises are meaningless, and I'm sleeping with the pool boy."
ADVANTAGE: Men's hoops

OFFICIALS:
MEN'S HOOPS: Refs
WOMEN'S HOOPS: Mediators
ADVANTAGE: Push. No one wins with the zebras, kids.

DO THEY DUNK?:
MEN'S HOOPS: Yes
WOMEN'S HOOPS: No, unless you count Puritan punishment for witches, and I do!
ADVANTAGE: Push

HOW THEY ARGUE WITH COACH:
MEN'S HOOPS: Choke him
WOMEN'S HOOPS: Pull her hair
ADVANTAGE: Push

TRASH TALK:
MEN'S HOOPS: "Get that weak **** out of my face!"
WOMEN'S HOOPS: "That sweatband is soooo last year!"
ADVANTAGE: Men's hoops

BLESSED WITH A GOD-GIVEN ABILITY TO:
MEN'S HOOPS: Fill the world with bad rap music
WOMEN'S HOOPS: Burst into tears
ADVANTAGE: Women's hoops

WHEN TEMPERS FLARE:
MEN'S HOOPS: It's a healthy sense of competition.
WOMEN'S HOOPS: Catfight! Catfight!
ADVANTAGE: Women's hoops

SECRET SHAME:
MEN'S HOOPS: Too scared to admit they don't "get" the triangle offense
WOMEN'S HOOPS: Too tall to date anyone in Hollywood
ADVANTAGE: Push

[So far, the men are winning in a dudeslide, but let's take the hoop blinders off and stack 'em up in the lightning round!]

GOT MILK?:
MEN: No
WOMEN: Yes!
ADVANTAGE: Women

CHILDREN BORNE:
MEN: 0
WOMEN: 6 billion
X | ADVANTAGE: Women

WOULD ACTUALLY WEAR A TV REMOTE HOLSTER:
WOMEN: No
MEN: Yes
X | ADVANTAGE: Men

SECRETLY HOPES SON GROWS UP TO BE:
WOMEN: Whatever truly makes him happy
MEN: Defensive back
ADVANTAGE: Men. You can't teach speed...

WHAT GRAY HAIR MEANS:
WOMEN: Father
MEN: Death
- - | ADVANTAGE: Push

MINDLESS RELAXATION WHILE WATCHING TV:
WOMEN: Needlepoint
MEN: Pinch 'n' roll
X | ADVANTAGE: Women

OFT-HEARD COMPLAINT:
WOMEN: Men don't know how to listen.
MEN: Huh?
X | ADVANTAGE: Women

HAS IN COMMON WITH KICKERS:
WOMEN: Sensitivity
MEN: Nothing
X | ADVANTAGE: Men

FAVORITE CATALOG:
WOMEN: Victoria's Secret
MEN: Victoria's Secret
X | ADVANTAGE: Men (You know...)

THINGS THAT DIDN'T WORK OUT:
WOMEN: Susan B. Anthony silver dollars
MEN: Government
X | ADVANTAGE: Women

CAN SAY "I LOVE YOU" IN HOW MANY LANGUAGES:
WOMEN: 2
MEN: 0
X | ADVANTAGE: Women

GENDER-EXCLUSIVE ANATOMY:
MEN: Extra rib
WOMEN: Uterus
X | ADVANTAGE: Women

NUMBER OF WHINY LETTERS I RECEIVE ABOUT MY DATA:
MEN: 0
WOMEN: 942
X | ADVANTAGE: *Women*

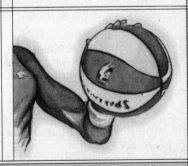

So there you have it; it's all so simple when you break things down scientifically. In a stunner, the advantage goes to women. I guess I'm feeling mixed emotions: As a man I mourn, yet my feminine side can't suppress a girlish giggle. But the really telling stat will be who has a sense of humor about this...What's that noise? Hmmm. Sounded like my wife closing a suitcase...Until next time, I'm Nick Bakay, reminding you the numbers never lie.

The noble premise of the WNBA is suffering from a basic fact: Most women will pass up *SportsCenter* for a rerun of *Veronica's Closet*. That's the way it is. I don't judge. As a man, I have been known to watch professional indoor lacrosse, just so I don't have to listen to those mewling yentas on *The View*. Regardless, without hulking manbutts filling the seats, a sport will always be small time unless it finds a way to get men to watch.

It's simple: contact. Hot girl-on-girl action. You know what I'm talking about—a point spread *and* that tingly feeling you get when the wife's asleep and Showtime's running a Shannon Tweed marathon. Femhoops may never achieve my agenda, but I think I know what will: Why not the WNFL?

I know a few fledgling semi-pro leagues and scattered high school outposts sport husky gals playing the game far from the spotlight, but I'm talking about hormonally altered professionals laying it all on the line on fourth and one. It gives a whole new meaning to the old football adage "Drive from the hips and buttocks."

Stick with me on this one, and Arena Football may have a girlfriend to help build the dream of year-round football. Of course, revolution is never easy. That's why we need to run a simple checklist, pros and cons, our own feasibility study, if you will...

WHY A WNFL?: If *The Jerry Springer Show* is any litmus test, women enjoy fighting.

WHY NOT?: Pregnant hillbilly strippers don't have the mental discipline to run the West Coast offense.

WHY A WNFL?: There is no such thing as bad football.

WHY NOT?: Can you imagine all the weeping?

WHY A WNFL?: The snap from center becomes illicit in a whole new way.

WHY NOT?: "I broke a nail!"

WHY A WNFL?: Women have a higher threshold for pain.

WHY NOT?: To date, no woman on Earth has been able to throw a spiral.

WHY A WNFL?: Some gals already dress like Vince Lombardi.

WHY NOT?: Hey, a lazy Y chromosome doesn't make you a leader, Missy!

WHY A WNFL?: Corporate sponsors will line up to target a female demographic.

WHY NOT?: "Good afternoon, ladies and gentlemen, and welcome to Vagisil Stadium!"

WHY A WNFL?: A slower game means less injuries.

WHY NOT?: Groin pulls eclipsed by bloating.

WHY A WNFL?: More TV work for sportscasters.

WHY NOT?: I can't quite picture the opening of the Monday night game when two huge napkins collide and explode.

WHY A WNFL?: Sisterhood is not a dirty word.

WHY NOT?: Once teammates get on the same cycle, look for a lot of punting on second down.

WHY A WNFL?: Tailgate food may actually now include a vegetable.

WHY NOT?: The only thing women bring to a tailgate party is whine.

WHY A WNFL?: Women get a shot at team ownership.

WHY NOT?: Women don't make good owners. Marge Schott. Georgia Frontiere. Art Modell. Am I right?

Still, the WNFL has five things going for it:

1) It's my idea.
2) Don't we all have a cousin named Lucy who seems born to play middle linebacker?
3) L.A. could actually get a team in this league!
4) I've got some nifty ideas for where Nike can put the swoosh.
5) All the sexual tension of a women's prison movie, and you can bet on it, too!

The WNFL: Women can feel emancipated, and men can feel naughty. Me? I love the ladies, and I'm just doing my part to level the playing field.

Ali and Frazier: The very names evoke bad blood out of the ring and bloodbaths inside it—which is exactly what the daughters of these two legends had in mind when Laila Ali and Jackie Frazier-Lyde slugged it out in Verona, New York. Ali prevailed in the end, but the big fun was looking ahead to this sideshow, which is exactly what I did right around Father's Day 2001.

Thought it might be fun to see a script in the same form we send to ESPN.

FYI: SOT means "sound on tape," or a video clip with sound. (PARENTHETICALS) include footage details as well as direction. For example: (COUGHING), which reminds Nick to summon up all his acting skills and cough on cue.

NICK: Do they have game, or just the name? (COUGHING) Sideshow! ...Sorry, I had something caught in my throat...(COUGHING) Shameless carnival act! (RECOVERING) I'm okay! I'm okay! Now, where was I? Ah, yes: Ali-Frazier 4: Will they hold a candle to their fathers' epic battles? Let's see how they stack up at the Tale of the Tape...

FATHERS DAUGHTERS

Nick Bakay's Tale of the Tape

ALI VS. FRAZIER IV: THE DAUGHTERS

PRE-FIGHT HYPE:
FATHERS: The Thrilla' in Manila!
DAUGHTERS: The Progesterone-a in Verona!
ADVANTAGE: Fathers

CAREER RECORDS:
FATHERS: Muhammad Ali: 56-5, Joe Frazier: 32-4-1
DAUGHTERS: Laila Ali: 9-0, Jackie Frazier-Lyde: 7-0, a combined total of 14 KOs between them, plus one controversial decision over a hermaphrodite
ADVANTAGE: Fathers

HIGHLIGHTS:
FATHERS: *(ANNOUNCER SOT: ALI-FRAZIER ACTION HIGHLIGHT)*
DAUGHTERS: *(OVER CLIP OF FRAZIER-LYDE: BELL RINGS, WOMEN RUN AT EACH OTHER, OPPONENT IS DROPPED WITH FIRST PUNCH 3 SECONDS IN)*
NICK: There's the bell for round one! And down goes the unemployed mother of three! Down goes the unemployed mother of three!
ADVANTAGE: Push, in a shocker
NICK: This time it's personal. Fathers?
SOT: *CLIP OF JOE AND ALI WRESTLING, WITH COSELL SAYING, "Sit down, Joe!"*

DAUGHTERS:
SOT #1: *Laila Ali: "I'm gonna get the loudmouth, annoying Jackie Frazier out of the way."*
SOT #2: *FRAZIER-LYDE: "I'm gonna break her face, okay?"*
NICK: Meow, somebody change the litter in their box...
ADVANTAGE: Daughters

TOUGHEST OPPONENTS:
FATHERS: Each other
DAUGHTERS: *(FOOTAGE: JACKIE FRAZIER FIGHTING HUGELY OUT OF SHAPE WOMAN)*
NICK: Was that Peter McNeely, or Aunt Bee? For God's sake, stop hitting Aunt Bee! "Oh Andy! I hurt!"
ADVANTAGE: Fathers

IN THEIR CORNERS:
FATHERS: Trainer, cut man, entourage
DAUGHTERS: Trainer, cut man, one dog-eared copy of *Chicken Soup for the Tomboy's Soul*
ADVANTAGE: Daughters

CELEBRITIES RINGSIDE:
FATHERS: Frank Sinatra
DAUGHTERS: Frank Sinatra Jr.
ADVANTAGE: Fathers

DO THEY WORK WITH PROPS?:
FATHERS: *(SOT: ALI WITH GORILLA DOLL: "Come on gorilla, we in Manila!")*
DAUGHTERS: *(FOOTAGE: JACKIE PUNCHING THROUGH A CAKE BAKED BY LAILA)*
NICK: Consider the action when Frazier was presented with a cake baked by Ali...Good form: You'll notice she punched through to the back of the cake's head.
ADVANTAGE: Daughters

BROADCASTS:
FATHERS: The old closed-circuit theaters
DAUGHTERS: Pay Per View, and a lipstick camera simultaneously feeding images to www.catfight.com.org
ADVANTAGE: Daughters

WE HAVE THEM TO THANK FOR:
FATHERS: Putting Don King on the map
DAUGHTERS: An under card featuring fighting roosters, some former XFL cheerleaders mud wrestling, and a couple of Bob Crane's home videos
ADVANTAGE: Push

WHAT WOULD MICHAEL BUFFER SAY?:
FATHERS: "LLLet's get ready to Rum..."—oh, that's right, I can't say it.
DAUGHTERS: "LLLet's get ready to pull each other's hair!"
X | ADVANTAGE: Daughters

DOES THE FIGHT FEATURE A HYPHENATED LAST NAME?:
FATHERS: No!
DAUGHTERS: Yes!
X | ADVANTAGE: Daughters

SECRET WISHES:
FATHERS: That they could still count to ten
DAUGHTERS: That somebody remembered to TiVo *The View*
ADVANTAGE: Push

THEY RANK RIGHT UP THERE WITH:
FATHERS: Louis-Schmelling
DAUGHTERS: Aguilera-Spears, "The Mayhem of the Midriff"
ADVANTAGE: Oh the hell with it...

So there you have it; it's all so simple when you break things down scientifically. In a sweet science sucker punch, the advantage...goes to Ali-Frazier, the next generation! Oh my goodness, the gals take it in a stunner! Color me a sentimental fool, but nothing says "Happy Father's Day" better than cracking a fresh can o' whup-ass and dumping it on the progeny of Dad's enemies. Until next time, I'm Nick Bakay, reminding you the numbers never lie...

The year they scheduled the ESPYs on Valentine's Day led to a request for Robin to take the wheel solo. Needless to say, mayhem ensued...

Like cartoon football helmets floating above the field, bucking and rearing for collision, so go the affairs of the heart and of the fans on February 14. Couples everywhere face a decision sure to induce behavior worse than Rocker's at the Museum of Tolerance. To gaze at the best in sports, or into the eyes of that special someone? Valentine's Day. ESPYs. Let's see how they stack up at the Tale of the Tape.

VALENTINE'S	ESPYS	
-	-	**WHERE IT'S AT:** VALENTINE'S DAY: Sofas all over the world ESPYS: Sin City, Nevada ADVANTAGE: Push
X		**WHAT IT'S ALL ABOUT:** VALENTINE'S DAY: A day to make love, not money ESPYS: A night to honor the "me" in team ADVANTAGE: Valentine's Day
-	-	**DO I HAVE TO?:** VALENTINE'S DAY: Men ESPYS: Women ADVANTAGE: Push
-	-	**PERKS:** VALENTINE'S DAY: If you have to ask... ESPYS: Bill Murray ADVANTAGE: Push
	X	**GUIDING PRINCIPLE:** VALENTINE'S DAY: Buy Hallmark cards ESPYS: Shameless self-promotion ADVANTAGE: ESPYs
	X	**PROPER ATTIRE:** VALENTINE'S DAY: Loose, easily removable garb ESPYS: Gamederpants! (Team Bakay patent pending.) ADVANTAGE: ESPYs

	X	**PILLOW TALK:** VALENTINE'S DAY: "Don't go there, boyfriend—that door's locked." ESPYS: "The winner couldn't be here tonight because he was indicted." ADVANTAGE: Valentine's Day
-	-	**GREAT EXPECTATIONS:** VALENTINE'S DAY: This year, no rashes! ESPYS: Michael Jackson thanks you—on air—for waving to him in Birmingham that time. ADVANTAGE: Push
-	-	**OUT-AND-OUT LIES:** VALENTINE'S DAY: "That looks sooo good on you." ESPYS: "Coming up next: Georgia Frontiere's flashdance." ADVANTAGE: Push
-	-	**TRICKLE-DOWN PROFITS:** VALENTINE'S DAY: Victoria's Secret ESPYS: Chinese takeout ADVANTAGE: Push
-	-	**CHECK, PLEASE:** VALENTINE'S DAY: "Do you like children?" ESPYS: "Give it up for Hootie & The Blowfish!" ADVANTAGE: Push
-	-	**YOU SHOULD BE SO LUCKY:** VALENTINE'S DAY: Next year's date—Nick Bakay! ESPYS: Next year's host—Nick Bakay! ADVANTAGE: Push

So there you have it; in a can't-we-all-just-get-along détente, the advantage goes to push. Take a big-screen TV, pass a good bottle of vino, and you've got sparkling entertainment—with especially relaxing commercial breaks. As Nick always says, the numbers never lie. Of course, he doesn't wear designer women's clothes...

RING-CARD GIRLS VS. MUD-FLAP GIRLS

RING CARD GIRLS
MUD-FLAP GIRLS

What is it about the female form that makes men idealize it? For some, that may mean the Venus de Milo, but I *likes* me a mud-flap girl. You're driving down the road, minding your own business, an eighteen-wheeler cuts you off…and you don't mind because you've fallen in love with the shapely silhouette arching her bare back above his rear tires. So what if she's a mere cartoon, I'd have a better chance with her than I would with, say, a ring-card girl parading around a heavyweight fight in a Budweiser bikini…Hey! That gives me an idea. Ring-card girls, mud-flap girls. Let's see how they stack up at the Tale of the Tape…

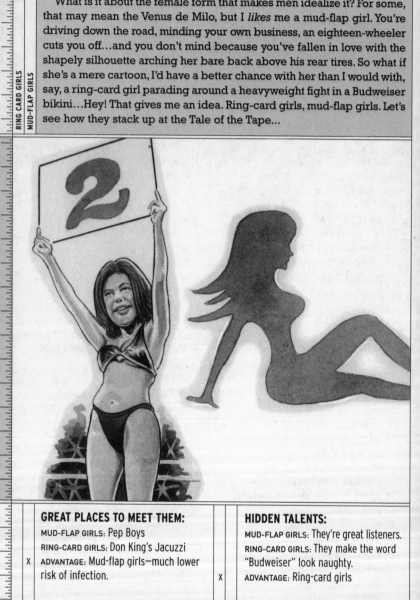

GREAT PLACES TO MEET THEM:
MUD-FLAP GIRLS: Pep Boys
RING-CARD GIRLS: Don King's Jacuzzi
X ADVANTAGE: Mud-flap girls—much lower risk of infection.

HIDDEN TALENTS:
MUD-FLAP GIRLS: They're great listeners.
RING-CARD GIRLS: They make the word "Budweiser" look naughty.
X ADVANTAGE: Ring-card girls

COMMUNITY SERVICE:
MUD-FLAP GIRLS: Protect us from the deadly spew of gravel.
RING-CARD GIRLS: Make sure we know what round we're in.
ADVANTAGE: Push—and did I mention I'm in love?

IF THEY HAD NAMES:
MUD-FLAP GIRLS: Road Rage
RING-CARD GIRLS: Cerveza
ADVANTAGE: Ring-card girls, in a squeaker

WHO BROKE THEIR HEARTS:
MUD-FLAP GIRLS: Karl Malone's truck
RING-CARD GIRLS: Michael "I'll call you" Buffer
ADVANTAGE: Push

ALL APPLICANTS MUST BE ABLE TO:
MUD-FLAP GIRLS: Sit in high heels, arching their backs
RING-CARD GIRLS: Strut in high heels, arching their backs
ADVANTAGE: Ring-card girls

KNOW THEIR WAY AROUND:
MUD-FLAP GIRLS: Route 80
RING-CARD GIRLS: The bowels of urban arenas
ADVANTAGE: Push

I SWEAR SHE SAID... :
MUD-FLAP GIRLS: "I'll follow you anywhere, honey."
RING-CARD GIRLS: "My dad's gonna win this fight."
ADVANTAGE: Mud-flap girls

IF SHE WERE MINE:
MUD-FLAP GIRLS: She'd only see me from behind.
RING-CARD GIRLS: She'd probably want kids.
ADVANTAGE: Push

ACCOLADES:
MUD-FLAP GIRLS: Tattooed on men's arms worldwide
RING-CARD GIRLS: Won Best Hostess at the Kansas City car show.
ADVANTAGE: Mud-flap girls

WHY I LOVE THEM:
MUD-FLAP GIRLS: They're all twins.
RING-CARD GIRLS: They keep me focused during under card.
ADVANTAGE: Mud-flap girls

PASTS:
MUD-FLAP GIRLS: Spent thirty years on the road with John Madden.
RING-CARD GIRLS: Frederick's of Hollywood "Thongs for the Memories!" catalog
ADVANTAGE: Ring-card girls

So there you have it; in a controversial decision that reeks of WBA-WBC corruption, the advantage goes to push. Sure, both are unattainable, but a guy can dream, can't he? Until next time, I'm Nick Bakay, reminding you the numbers never lie.

COURTING FREE AGENTS VS. COURTING SVETLANA

What do general managers have in common with guys searching the Internet for Russian women to marry? They both think they can buy hope for their shredded dreams. Import a quarterback, import a bride, both know they can't do it alone anymore. The GM wines and dines a hot free agent and prays he doesn't discover the dearth of Porsche dealerships in the area, while Lonely McLoner e-mails an impossibly beautiful woman a ten-year-old photo of himself, along with a list of reasons why she should leave Minsk for a pickup truck and his dogs in northern Minnesota. With any luck, the GM gets a star on his roster, and Lonely gets someone to kick him when he snores. Courting free agents. Courting Svetlana. Let's see how they stack up at the Tale of the Tape.

FREE AGENTS | SVETLANA

WHY YOU FLEW THEM IN:
FREE AGENT: To goose ticket sales
SVETLANA: To goose your sorry ass
X ADVANTAGE: Svetlana

THE LAST TIME... :
FREE AGENT: You made the play-offs, people still liked Ike.
SVETLANA: You had sex, you had to pay for it.
-- ADVANTAGE: Push

CHALLENGES:
FREE AGENT: Selling the "virtues" of your city's tendency to have snow in April
SVETLANA: Teaching her the English word for "tampon"
-- ADVANTAGE: Push

AIRPORT SURPRISES:
FREE AGENT: He brought along "Booger," his personal advisor/homey.
SVETLANA: In her picture, she's a tall, willowy blonde. In person, she's a dead ringer for James Gandolfini.
X ADVANTAGE: Free agent

HOW YOU MET:
FREE AGENT: His agent called at 12:01 A.M. on the first day of free agency.
SVETLANA: You logged on to russianbeautease.com.
X ADVANTAGE: Svetlana

WHY THEY'RE LOOKING FOR A NEW HOME:

FREE AGENT: Felt dissed by his old team's $50 million offer.

SVETLANA: Tired of rotating summer and winter babushkas.

X | ADVANTAGE: Svetlana

PERKS:

FREE AGENT: A generous signing bonus

SVETLANA: New brother-in-law-to-be is a hunk.

X | ADVANTAGE: Free agent

WHAT IT'S GOING TO TAKE TO GET A DEAL DONE:

FREE AGENT: A Rolls, a soup commercial for his mother, and a role in the next Vin Diesel movie

SVETLANA: An IRA, a Victoria's Secret credit card, and some cattle

X | ADVANTAGE: Svetlana

WELCOMING COMMITTEE:

FREE AGENT: Owner, head coach, team captains

SVETLANA: You, and a hastily purchased Vermont Teddy Bear

X | ADVANTAGE: Free agent

SQUEEZE 'EM TIGHT:

FREE AGENT: His salary under the cap

SVETLANA: Tins of caviar into suitcase to sell in America

- - | ADVANTAGE: Push

UH-OH:

FREE AGENT: The league just called about his last urine test.

SVETLANA: Immigration wants to question her about the caviar.

- - | ADVANTAGE: Push

HIDDEN AGENDA:

FREE AGENT: A voidable fourth year

SVETLANA: A green card

X | ADVANTAGE: Svetlana

OOPS:

FREE AGENT: Thought "Malevolence" was a member of the Justice League of America.

SVETLANA: Your name is Dougy, but she keeps pronouncing it "Douchie."

X | ADVANTAGE: Free agent

DEAL BREAKERS:

FREE AGENT: The morals clause

SVETLANA: The goat stays

X | ADVANTAGE: Svetlana

TOUGH SELLS:

FREE AGENT: Explaining how he's going to post great stats behind an all-rookie lie

SVETLANA: Explaining that your "mansion by the sea" is really "a trailer in the woods"

- - | ADVANTAGE: Push

IF EVERYTHING WORKS OUT:

FREE AGENT: He'll sign before he leaves town and lead you to a championship.

SVETLANA: She'll sign, you'll fix her teeth, and she'll give birth to the next Johnny Unitas.

X | ADVANTAGE: Svetlana

So there you have it; it's so simple when you break things down scientifically. On a top-shelf-where-Mamma-hides-the-beers-and-blinis squeaker, the advantage goes to Svetlana, provided she stops downloading all those David Hasselhoff MP3s. Until next time, I'm Nick Bakay, reminding you the numbers never lie.

When it comes to propaganda, Chairman Mao had nothing on NFL films. The Wagnerian music, the basso profundo of John Facenda—no one did a better job of sating a male audience hungry for vicarious glory...until we all fell asleep in front of the TV, only to awake at 2 A.M. to the camcorder voyeurism that is *Girls Gone Wild*. It's time to settle the question of A.V. Squad supremacy once and for all. NFL films versus *GGW*, the crackle of fall vs. spring break, let's see how they stack up at the Tale of the Tape...

Nick Bakay's Tale of the Tape

SIGNATURE SHOTS:
NFL FILMS: A running back speeding down the sideline, his helmet bobbing in super slo-mo
GIRLS GONE WILD: A freckled coed raising her tank top over her head without snagging it on her Mardi Gras beads
ADVANTAGE: Um...push?

SOUND BITES:
NFL FILMS: "There's a gleam, men! There's a gleam!"
GIRLS GONE WILD: "I...I've never done this before."
ADVANTAGE: Um...push?

GREAT FILMS ARE BUILT IN THE EDITING ROOM:
NFL FILMS: "Do we have any shots of Al Davis without the sunglasses?"
GIRLS GONE WILD: "We can cut around the part where she blows chunks."
ADVANTAGE: Um...push?

WHAT YOU NEVER HEAR:
NFL FILMS: "The once-famous quarterback eventually found himself with his best friend and children no longer by his side, drinking heavily, and contemplating the pregnant diner waitress on the mattresses beneath the frozen window."
GIRLS GONE WILD: "I can't. It's Sabbath."
ADVANTAGE: *Girls Gone Wild*

POETRY:
NFL FILMS: "The autumn wind is a Raider..."
GIRLS GONE WILD: "The rustle in your pants is a sophomore."
ADVANTAGE: Push—either way, you're swaggering boisterously.

GODHEADS:
NFL FILMS: Lombardi
GIRLS GONE WILD: Mandy
ADVANTAGE: Push! Wow! Kudos, Mandy!

MECCAS:
NFL FILMS: Canton, Ohio
GIRLS GONE WILD: Bourbon Street
ADVANTAGE: *GGW*

RAISON D'ETRE:
NFL FILMS: Glory
GIRLS GONE WILD: Goo
ADVANTAGE: *GGW*—Goo does not preclude glory.

MORAL QUAGMIRES:
NFL FILMS: "Say what you want, but that O.J. could run!"
GIRLS GONE WILD: "Oh yeah...Oh yeah...Oh my God, that's my daughter!"
ADVANTAGE: Push, and shame on you.

WHERE ELSE CAN YOU SEE:
NFL FILMS: The immaculate reception from three different angles
GIRLS GONE WILD: Your babysitter's aureoles
ADVANTAGE: Push

CAN PUT A POSITIVE SPIN ON:
NFL FILMS: The 2003 Bengals: "Not half as sucky as we expected!"
GIRLS GONE WILD: The exploitation of young women who have only recently discovered tequila
ADVANTAGE: Push

UNLIKELY HEROES:
NFL FILMS: Steve Sabol
GIRLS GONE WILD: The blonde twins making out on the Seadoo
ADVANTAGE: *GGW*

WHAT YOU SAY WHEN YOUR WIFE FINDS THE DVD:

NFL FILMS: "Hey, I don't give you crap when *Sex and the City* is on!"

GIRLS GONE WILD: "How the hell did *that* get in here?"

And personally, if *my* wife finds the DVD, I'd say, "Thank you."

ADVANTAGE: Me!

VIEWER PROFILE:

NFL FILMS: 5' 8", 279 lbs., hasn't run ten consecutive yards since the Reagan administration

GIRLS GONE WILD: 5' 8", 279 lbs., hasn't been touched by a woman since he "accidentally" brushed against that gal on the bus

ADVANTAGE: Push

THE PRICE YOU PAY:

NFL FILMS: $17.99

GIRLS GONE WILD: Your dignity and/or your current relationship

ADVANTAGE: NFL Films

WHEN IT'S OVER, YOU FEEL... :

NFL FILMS: Ready to lift a car over your head

GIRLS GONE WILD: Tired, sad, and alone

ADVANTAGE: NFL Films

ATTEMPTS AT LEVITY:

NFL FILMS: Football Follies—the gut-busting hilarity that is sixty minutes of punters slipping in mud

GIRLS GONE WILD: DVD extra—"Weeping Angry Boyfriends"

ADVANTAGE: *GGW*

WHEN THEY PUT A MICROPHONE ON THE PLAYERS:

NFL FILMS: "This is when the big dogs eat!"

GIRLS GONE WILD: "Don't I get a free T-shirt?"

ADVANTAGE: NFL Films

FOR THOSE WHO DELIGHT IN:

NFL FILMS: The abuse of others

GIRLS GONE WILD: The abuse of self

ADVANTAGE: NFL Films

THE BEST THING NEXT TO:

NFL FILMS: A real game

GIRLS GONE WILD: A real woman, or at least XXX porn

ADVANTAGE: NFL Films

GIVES NEW MEANING TO THE PHRASE:

NFL FILMS: Tundra

GIRLS GONE WILD: Raw footage

ADVANTAGE: Push

So there you have it; it's all so easy when you break things down scientifically. In the kinda tie that makes kissing your sister kinda hot, the advantage goes to push. Screw AFI, the perfect DVD library contains more of these two, less *Annie Hall*. Until next time, I'm Nick Bakay, reminding you the numbers never lie.

Now & Then

LOU GEHRIG VS. CAL RIPKEN

GEHRIG
RIPKEN

How fair is it to compare an iron man of the nineties to an iron man of the 1920s? Isn't this really about who had a harder time staying in there for 2,130 games? Who had a steeper degree of difficulty? About who had the *dis*advantage? Lou Gehrig, Cal Ripken, let's see how they stack up at the Tale of the Tape...

WEAR AND TEAR OF POSITION:
RIPKEN: Shortstop
GEHRIG: First base
X   DISADVANTAGE: Ripken

NUMBER OF STRIKE DAYS HE WAS ALLOWED TO REST:
RIPKEN: 228
GEHRIG: 0
X   DISADVANTAGE: Gehrig

GAME DAY TRANSPORTATION:
RIPKEN: Limo to chartered plane to four-star hotel
GEHRIG: Rickshaw to steamboat to donkey
X   DISADVANTAGE: Gehrig

SALARY:
RIPKEN: Guaranteed millions
GEHRIG: An honest wage and the occasional dill pickle
X   DISADVANTAGE: Gehrig

TRAINING ROOM SUPPLIES:
RIPKEN: Whirlpool, MRI, hyperbaric chamber
GEHRIG: Dr. Injun's magical tonic elixir
X   DISADVANTAGE: Gehrig

MOST FAMOUS QUOTE:
GEHRIG: "Today I consider myself the luckiest man in the world."
RIPKEN: "Mentos IS the freshmaker!"
X   DISADVANTAGE: Ripken!

MEDICAL BELIEFS OF THE DAY:
RIPKEN: A balanced diet and complex amino acids will keep you fit and boost energy.
GEHRIG: Leeches will bleed out the bad stuff, or we can cut a hole in your skull to let the hobgoblins out of your soul...
X   DISADVANTAGE: Gehrig

GOT HIS JOB:
GEHRIG: When he worked his way into the Yankee lineup
RIPKEN: When his dad worked for the Orioles
X   DISADVANTAGE: Gehrig

DESTINATION AFTER SETTING RECORD:
RIPKEN: Disneyland
GEHRIG: Hospital
X   DISADVANTAGE: Gehrig

BEHIND-THE-SCENES CHALLENGE:
RIPKEN: Had to play through his dad's firing
GEHRIG: Had to play through Babe Ruth's beer farts
X   DISADVANTAGE: Gehrig

WAYS OF RELAXING ON THE ROAD:
RIPKEN: Video games, cell phone, cable TV
GEHRIG: Whorin' with the Babe
– –   DISADVANTAGE: Push...

And finally:

REASON FOR FINALLY MISSING A GAME:
RIPKEN: Onset of ennui having already broken the record
GEHRIG: A terminal illness so horrible it was named after him
X   ADVANTAGE: Gehrig

So there you have it; it's so simple when you break things down scientifically. In a moral victory, the colossal disadvantage goes to Lou Gehrig. How could it be any other way? Until next time I'm Nick Bakay, reminding you the numbers never lie.

Who likes short shorts? Apparently not the NBA, where the hemlines would be appropriate at a Mennonite social, unlike the NBA of the seventies, when hot pants ruled the day. The infantilism of long shorts versus the visible panty line of short shorts—let's see how they stack up at the Tale of the Tape...

LONG
SHORT

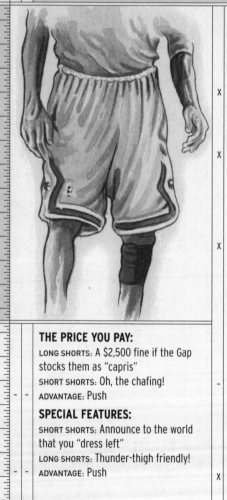

REMINISCENT OF:
LONG SHORTS: The guitar player for AC/DC
SHORT SHORTS: Bruce Jenner in "Can't Stop the Music"
X ADVANTAGE: Long shorts

ADJECTIVES:
LONG SHORTS: Breezy...
SHORT SHORTS: Snug
X ADVANTAGE: Long shorts, in a squeaker.

MEASUREMENTS:
LONG SHORTS: At least an inch above the knee
SHORT SHORTS: At least an inch below the grapes
X ADVANTAGE: Long shorts

FOUNDING FATHERS:
LONG SHORTS: Michigan's Fab Five
SHORT SHORTS: Hooters waitresses
X ADVANTAGE: Short shorts

FANS GET TO SEE:
LONG SHORTS: Underpants waistband
SHORT SHORTS: Hairy man-thighs. Who remembers Ernie DiGregorio?
- - ADVANTAGE: Push, no winners here.

FINES GO TO:
LONG SHORTS: The families of players who were injured tripping over their own pants on a fast break
SHORT SHORTS: Infertility clinics
X ADVANTAGE: Long shorts

THE PRICE YOU PAY:
LONG SHORTS: A $2,500 fine if the Gap stocks them as "capris"
SHORT SHORTS: Oh, the chafing!
- - ADVANTAGE: Push

SPECIAL FEATURES:
SHORT SHORTS: Announce to the world that you "dress left"
LONG SHORTS: Thunder-thigh friendly!
- - ADVANTAGE: Push

THE TRADITIONAL PAT ON THE POPO BECOMES:
SHORT SHORTS: A vast source of information
LONG SHORTS: An Easter egg hunt
ADVANTAGE: Push

ADVANTAGES:
LONG SHORTS: Great for shoplifting
SHORT SHORTS: The space available for tattoos
ADVANTAGE: Long shorts

DISADVANTAGES:
LONG SHORTS: Your own clothes can actually defend a behind-the-back pass.
SHORT SHORTS: Not a good look for Shaq
ADVANTAGE: Push

MADE BY:
LONG SHORTS: Nike
SHORT SHORTS: International Male
ADVANTAGE: Long shorts

So there you have it; it's so simple when you break things down scientifically. In a junk-in-the-trunk showdown, the advantage goes to long shorts! But ultimately, are there any winners when we talk about grown men wearing shorts to work? Until next time, I'm Nick Bakay, reminding you the numbers never lie.

FIRST SIGNING BONUS VS. LAST SIGNING BONUS

FIRST BONUS | **LAST BONUS**

Big, fat, juicy signing bonuses—something most of us can only dream of. Oh sure, you could ask for one, only to hear, "Your bonus is you get to come back to work again tomorrow." In the world of professional sports, however, seven-figure bonuses are the norm, along with easily reached performance bonuses like $250,000 for waking up every morning in the month of May. It's a sweet deal, but big money can bring a galaxy of problems, and a pro athlete's earning years are precious and few. For those who actually survive long enough to earn a first bonus and a last bonus, let's see how they stack up at the Tale of the Tape...

PAYOUT:
FIRST BONUS: Prorated over five years
LAST BONUS: Reworked for cap space so often, you'll see the last check in 2056
ADVANTAGE: First bonus

BIG-TICKET ITEMS:
FIRST BONUS: Buy a house for Mom.
LAST BONUS: Buy a house for all seven women you impregnated but didn't marry.
ADVANTAGE: First bonus

WHAT THE TEAM IS BANKING ON:
FIRST BONUS: You'll fulfill your promise and make them look like geniuses.
LAST BONUS: You'll be cut before next year's balloon payment.
ADVANTAGE: First bonus

YOUR RIDE:
FIRST BONUS: Hummer, Ferrari, Escalade, Porsche
LAST BONUS: Car service since that fifth DUI
ADVANTAGE: First bonus

OUTLOOK:
FIRST BONUS: The second contract is when you'll make the monster green.
LAST BONUS: I'm twenty-eight, and this money has to last until I die.
ADVANTAGE: First bonus

INVESTMENTS:
FIRST BONUS: Paternity insurance
LAST BONUS: Going to court to reduce your alimony
ADVANTAGE: Push

YOU'VE GOT YOUR EYE ON:
FIRST BONUS: A vacation trip
LAST BONUS: A shiny new hip
ADVANTAGE: First bonus

PAYBACK'S A BITCH:
FIRST BONUS: All those "loans" from college boosters
LAST BONUS: All that commission you owe your agent
ADVANTAGE: Push

NOW YOU WISH YOU'D:
FIRST BONUS: Majored in economics, not Phys ed.
LAST BONUS: Said no to that "can't miss" alpaca farm deal.
ADVANTAGE: Last bonus. I hear they make great pets.

EXPENSIVE HABITS:
FIRST BONUS: Posting bail for your posse
LAST BONUS: Your recent bout of "fumble-itis"
ADVANTAGE: Push

BAD ADVICE:
FIRST BONUS: Giving us power of attorney lets you focus on the game!
LAST BONUS: Jaromir Jagr swears he's found a way to avoid paying taxes by gambling on-line!
ADVANTAGE: Push

BLING-BLING:
FIRST BONUS: Two-carat studs in your front teeth
LAST BONUS: Two championship rings on eBay
ADVANTAGE: Push

DIVERSIFICATION:
FIRST BONUS: Blondes and brunettes
LAST BONUS: Bonds and REITS
ADVANTAGE: Push

YOU NEVER DREAMED:
FIRST BONUS: You would own two solid gold Foo dogs.
LAST BONUS: You would own stock in two bankrupt dot-coms.
ADVANTAGE: Push—just try to resell either.

LOVE AND MONEY:
FIRST BONUS: Spreading cash all over a bed and making love on it
LAST BONUS: Hiding cash where your common-law wife can't find it
ADVANTAGE: First bonus

BAD NEWS:
FIRST BONUS: According to your last tax return, you spent $568,000 on sunglasses.
LAST BONUS: According to your last team physical, you have the knees of a cadaver.
ADVANTAGE: Push

BEWARE:
FIRST BONUS: A luxury once tasted becomes a necessity.
LAST BONUS: A first-round pick at your position becomes extinct.
ADVANTAGE: Push

So there you have it; it's all so simple when you break things down scientifically. In a future-beats-a-past pasting, the advantage goes to the first signing bonus. But hang in there you last bonus pensioners, a golden parachute pretty much defines the concept of a classy problem, and if you really want to break out in a cold sweat, try retiring on a teacher's salary. Until next time, I'm Nick Bakay, reminding you the numbers never lie.

SNOWBOARDING SKIING

Numerous ski communities have their panties in a bunch over the number of snowboards popping up at their local chairlift. Could it be a changing of the guard? Skiing in America was always an elitist sport until Gen-X knocked it off its pedestal, but aren't both parties just looking for some powder and a slick piece of wood to carve it up? Can't we all just get along? Skiing, snowboarding, let's see how they stack up at the Tale of the Tape.

TYPICAL RUN NAMES:
SKIERS: The Copper Bowl, Little Nell, Blazing Star
BOARDERS: Dog Bone, The Worm, Pancreas
ADVANTAGE: Boarders

AVERAGE INCOME:
SKIERS: One hundred grand a year and up
BOARDERS: Whatever Starbucks pays
ADVANTAGE: Skiers

COMMON NICKNAMES:
SKIERS: Choo Choo, Bumper, and Scoot
BOARDERS: Rebel, Cutter, and Blister
ADVANTAGE: Push

THINKS BLUES TRAVELER IS:
BOARDERS: A band
SKIERS: A rash
ADVANTAGE: Boarders

TASTE IN LEADING MEN:
SKIERS: Mel, Harrison, and Sean
BOARDERS: SpongeBob, a Crank Yanker, and Silent Bob
ADVANTAGE: Too close to call, I'm sorry.

LAST RECORD PURCHASED:
BOARDERS: Butt Trumpet
SKIERS: *Mamma Mia!* soundtrack
ADVANTAGE: Boarders

WEB SITES:
BOARDERS: Flakezine
SKIERS: A hip replacement chat room
ADVANTAGE: Snowboarders

POTENT POTABLE:
SKIERS: A kier royale
BOARDERS: A microbrewed wheat beer
ADVANTAGE: Boarders

THINKS CROSS-COUNTRY SKIING IS... :
SKIERS: "Shhuper!"
BOARDERS: Almost as boring as a Nordic track
ADVANTAGE: Boarders

JUDGING CRITERIA:
SKIERS: Speed and form
BOARDERS: Amplitude, spiritual awareness, 'nads
ADVANTAGE: Boarders

WHAT THEIR CLOTHES SAY:
SKIERS: I'm thin, and I belong.
BOARDERS: I'm chubby and I don't care.
ADVANTAGE: No winners here

PERSONAL EXPRESSION:
BOARDERS: Tattoos and body piercing
SKIERS: Face-lifts and hair plugs
ADVANTAGE: Skiers. Ten years ago, I would have said snowboarders.

PARTICIPANTS:
SKIERS: Hoi polloi
BOARDERS: Lost youth
ADVANTAGE: Boarders

FREQUENT INJURIES:
SKIERS: Broken leg
BOARDERS: Infected Prince Albert pierce
ADVANTAGE: Skiers

COMMON ADVICE:
SKIERS: Bend your knees
BOARDERS: Paaaarty!
X ADVANTAGE: Skiers, because you don't always get a second chance to bend your knees.

MARTYRS:
SKIERS: Spider Savich
BOARDERS: Kurt Cobain
- - ADVANTAGE: Push

WIPEOUTS:
SKIERS: The agony of defeat
BOARDERS: The bummer of humiliation
- - ADVANTAGE: Push

HOW ONE STOPS
SKIERS: Snowplow
BOARDERS: Cold turkey
X ADVANTAGE: Skiers

DREAM VACATION:
BOARDERS: Vietnam with three crazy Danish dudes you met at a youth hostel
SKIERS: Aspen with the wife, the kids, and the buxom nanny
- - ADVANTAGE: Push

GLOSSARY:
SKIERS: Shush, stem, snowplow
BOARDERS: Boned, nose bonk, stinky
X ADVANTAGE: Boarders

HOW THEY SLEEP:
BOARDERS: In the nude
SKIERS: In fear of being poor
X ADVANTAGE: Boarders

So there you have it; it's all so simple when you break things down scientifically. In a grudge match, the advantage goes to snowboarding. Any sport that used to be called Snurfing can't be all bad. Until next time, I'm Nick Bakay, reminding you the numbers never lie.

SUPERSTAR VS. ROOKIE

Pitchers and catchers: In jail, it's a lifestyle. In baseball, it means the start of a new season. For players, it means one of two things—you're a superstar assured of a roster slot and easing into the grind, or you're a rookie on the bubble with little bank and lots to prove. But who really has the best ride in baseball's lazy, hazy warm up? Superstars, rookies—let's see how they stack up at the Tale of the Tape...

MOST POPULAR EXPECTORATION:

SUPERSTAR: Scrawking amber tobacco juice between pitches

ROOKIE: Blowing chunks through your mask the first time you have to catch Randy Johnson

ADVANTAGE: Push

REACTION TO BEING IN A BIG-LEAGUE CLUBHOUSE:

SUPERSTAR: Tip the clubhouse attendant $100 to swab your ears.

ROOKIE: "Golly! Take a look at all this here free gum!"

ADVANTAGE: Push. *Any* luxury once tasted becomes a necessity.

TYPICAL PLAYER RÉSUMÉS:

SUPERSTAR: Led majors in slugging percentage

ROOKIE: Drove a Coors truck

ADVANTAGE: Superstar

SHORTSTOPS:

SUPERSTAR: Goes to his right well.

ROOKIE: Goes to his right well for a guy with the foot speed of Louie Anderson.

ADVANTAGE: Superstar

FOR THE LOVE OF GOD, NEVER:

SUPERSTAR: Let them know you cork your bat.

ROOKIE: Point out the remarkable sag of the skipper's plum sack.

ADVANTAGE: Push. And let's please move on...

WHAT YOU SECRETLY FEAR THEY'LL FIND OUT:

SUPERSTAR: That you don't know what "K" means.

ROOKIE: You can't read.

ADVANTAGE: Push—neither has prevented anyone from playing Major League Baseball.

THE BOTTOM LINE:

SUPERSTAR: Between taxes, agent, and child support, your take-home on $7 million is actually $47 bucks.

ROOKIE: Maybe if I save up my per diem, I can buy new underpants.

ADVANTAGE: Superstar

WHAT TO PACK:

SUPERSTAR: Just enough jewelry to get you through the month

ROOKIE: Bus fare home

ADVANTAGE: Superstar

DINNER:

SUPERSTAR: "You can't find good sushi in Port St. Lucie."

ROOKIE: "This is the best damn Blimpies *ever*!"

ADVANTAGE: Rookie

LIP SERVICE:
SUPERSTAR: Everyone tells the press the fifty pounds you gained in the off-season will melt away by June.
ROOKIE: Everyone reassures you not to worry they assigned you uniform #273.
ADVANTAGE: Push

TYPICAL FEEDBACK FROM THE COACHING STAFF:
SUPERSTAR: "Please don't get me fired."
ROOKIE: "Son, have you ever considered farming?"
ADVANTAGE: Push

YA GOTTA PLAY HURT:
SUPERSTAR: Fouling a meaningless game ball off your foot
ROOKIE: Your townie girlfriend just dumped you for her cousin, Dupree.
ADVANTAGE: Dupree

IT'S WORTH GOING THROUGH THE HARD PARTS BECAUSE:
SUPERSTAR: There are no hard parts.
ROOKIE: Even bull pen catchers make seven figures a year.
ADVANTAGE: Push

RECREATIONAL TRANSPORTATION:
SUPERSTAR: Rent a Caddy and go to Hooters!
ROOKIE: Borrow a Schwinn and go tip cows.
ADVANTAGE: Superstar

IF YOU MAKE IT, YOU CAN LOOK FORWARD TO:
SUPERSTAR: Cleaning up at card shows well into your nineties
ROOKIE: Finally not being referred to as a thirty-two-year-old rookie
ADVANTAGE: Push

So there you have it; it's all so simple when you break things down scientifically. In a blowout, the advantage goes to superstars. No shock there, but think about it this way, rookie—getting released means you're one step closer to a job with a dental plan. Until next time, I'm Nick Bakay, reminding you the numbers never lie.

OLD SCHOOL **NEW SCHOOL**

No game keeps raising its style points like the NBA, yet in a world of entourages and $100 million deals, it's important to remember that the game's old school roots were built on two-handed bounce passes. Are things really better now that we've traded peach baskets for Plexiglas? Old school hoops versus the new school, let's see how they stack up at the Tale of the Tape...

BALL MOVEMENT:
OLD SCHOOL: Cycling the rock to the open man
NEW SCHOOL: An unfortunate side effect of hugely oversized pants
ADVANTAGE: Old school

DISTINGUISHING MARKS:
NEW SCHOOL: A unique tattoo of Asian symbols, which translate to "stupid," "dog," "porridge"
OLD SCHOOL: A unique cluster of head scars where your brush-cut won't grow
ADVANTAGE: Push

THE PROBLEM WITH SUPERSTARS:
OLD SCHOOL: Can we outbid that offer from the Globetrotters?
NEW SCHOOL: Will he make bail in time for tip-off?
ADVANTAGE: Old school

COURTSIDE DISTRACTIONS:
OLD SCHOOL: Hoping your wife and your girlfriend aren't seated in the same section
NEW SCHOOL: Calvin Klein keeps chirping, "Yoo-hoo! Mr. Sprewell!"
ADVANTAGE: Old school

Nick Bakay's Tale of the Tape

CLOSED-DOOR MEETINGS:

OLD SCHOOL: Where players air out their differences

NEW SCHOOL: Where players air out their pants at a strip club in Atlanta

ADVANTAGE: Push

YOU WILL BE FINED FOR THAT:

OLD SCHOOL: Showing up late

NEW SCHOOL: Answering your pager in the time-out huddle

X ADVANTAGE: Old school

COMMUNICATING WITH THE COACH:

OLD SCHOOL: Gaining possession and calling a time-out

NEW SCHOOL: Leaving purple ligature marks on his throat

ADVANTAGE: Push

WHERE THE MONEY GOES:

OLD SCHOOL: Food, rent

NEW SCHOOL: Child support, bling-bling, more child support

X ADVANTAGE: Old school

GETTING BENCHED:

OLD SCHOOL: A humiliating punishment

NEW SCHOOL: A chance to fire up the Palm Pilot and check out your bio-med stocks

X ADVANTAGE: New school

FOOTWEAR:

OLD SCHOOL: Regulation Chuck Taylors with a heaping dose of gym stank

NEW SCHOOL: Signature Nikes with state-of-the-art "Stank-B-Gone" technology

X ADVANTAGE: New school

ACTS OF HUMILIATION:

NEW SCHOOL: Hanging from the rim for the entire second half

OLD SCHOOL: Keeping your hands cocked in the shooting position three seconds after draining a shot

ADVANTAGE: Push—there are no winners when taunting rears its ugly head. Let's just play the game, fellas.

PLAYER INTRODUCTIONS:

NEW SCHOOL: House lights down, lasers up

OLD SCHOOL: The loud fart of the game horn

ADVANTAGE: Push

HOTDOGGING:

NEW SCHOOL: The no-look pass

OLD SCHOOL: Extra-super-fancy dribbling

X ADVANTAGE: New school

THE UGLY SIDE OF OWNER/PLAYER RELATIONS:

OLD SCHOOL: Second-hand cigar smoke

NEW SCHOOL: Mark Cuban just got his fourth technical

X ADVANTAGE: Old school

So there you have it; it's so simple when you break things down scientifically. In a player mutiny, the advantage goes to the new school. Let's face it, at the end of the day they give guys like me more to rag on. But hang in there, old school—you get the dreaded vote of confidence. Until next time, I'm Nick Bakay, reminding you the numbers never lie.

It may be the House That Ruth Built, but face it—it's in the Bronx. Forget Jeffrey Maier, the biggest nuisance for those attending a Yankee Stadium twi-nighter is that pesky "survival" thing. After years of threatening a move to the Yuppie West Side, or worse, Joisey, Steinbrenner is considering extending his lease well into this millennium. Of course, getting a vote of confidence from George is like going fishing with the Corleones. Still, if he's planning to stay, you gotta think the Boss has improvements in mind that will lure all those fat cats who've given up on the Knicks. Yes, we have to confront the real possibility that there will soon be a souped-up ballpark standing amid the rubble. Today's Yankee Stadium versus the stadium of tomorrow. Let's see how they stack up at the Tale of the Tape.

YOUR TICKET ENTITLES YOU TO:
OLD YANKEE STADIUM: Entry
NEW YANKEE STADIUM: Entry *and* a decent shot at exiting
ADVANTAGE: New

SECURITY:
OLD YANKEE STADIUM: Safe as a mesh condom.
NEW YANKEE STADIUM: Safe—as long as you stay within the confines of our bulletproof loge.
ADVANTAGE: New

POPULAR STADIUM TREAT:
OLD YANKEE STADIUM: Hot dogs
NEW YANKEE STADIUM: Sashimi fritters
ADVANTAGE: Old. No one wins when you go eclectic.

SEATS COME WITH:
OLD YANKEE STADIUM: Spent slugs
NEW YANKEE STADIUM: Individual latte caddies
ADVANTAGE: Old

PROMOTIONS:
OLD YANKEE STADIUM: Santeria Night
NEW YANKEE STADIUM: Stepkids' Night
ADVANTAGE: Old

FLY-BY BANNERS:
OLD YANKEE STADIUM: "Come out, come out, wherever you are."
NEW YANKEE STADIUM: "CATS—NOW and FOREVER"
ADVANTAGE: Push

HOUSE BAND:
OLD YANKEE STADIUM: Some oldster with a snoot full, a doughnut pillow, and a lead foot on the sustain pedal
NEW YANKEE STADIUM: Whoever Jeter's turning the DP with this week
ADVANTAGE: Old

HOUSE SLOGAN:
OLD YANKEE STADIUM: A tie—Up Yours/Bite Me
NEW YANKEE STADIUM: SuperSize It!
ADVANTAGE: Old

PUBLIC NUISANCES:
OLD YANKEE STADIUM: Derelicts offering to spit-clean your windshield for a quarter. And Phil Rizzuto.
NEW YANKEE STADIUM: Derelicts offering to spit-clean your windshield for a PSL. And Phil Rizzuto.
ADVANTAGE: Old

MONUMENT TO:
OLD YANKEE STADIUM: The Yankee legends: Babe, Gehrig, Joe D, the Mick...
NEW YANKEE STADIUM: Graft
ADVANTAGE: Old

GHOSTS:
OLD YANKEE STADIUM: Billy Martin
NEW YANKEE STADIUM: David Wells
ADVANTAGE: Push

"THE BOSS" LOOK:

OLD YANKEE STADIUM: White turtleneck, blue blazer

NEW YANKEE STADIUM: Leather shorts, tongue stud

X ADVANTAGE: New

COMMUTER RISKS:

OLD YANKEE STADIUM: Getting TB from a panhandler on the 4 train

NEW YANKEE STADIUM: Getting caught in gun crossfire and having to use your mistress as a human shield

X ADVANTAGE: Old

So there you have it; it's all so simple when you break things down scientifically. In a nod to tradition, the advantage goes to today's Yankee Stadium. I put in my time in the Big Apple, and as any New Yorker will tell you—if you want to see glistening facilities juxtaposed with lethal squalor, you're better off heading down to Atlantic City. Until next time, I'm Nick Bakay, reminding you the numbers never lie.

I CAN SEE IT NOW: "THE BALLPARK AT MEXICAN QUAALUDE YARDS"

While we're on the subject of stadiums and progress, did you catch this little item that stumbled, bleary-eyed, off the news wire?

English soccer club Witton Albion recently signed a sponsorship deal with a beverage store chain. From now on, the team's home field will be called...

BARGAIN BOOZE STADIUM.

Finally, a corporate sponsor we can all live with in an era where evocative names like Candlestick Park have faded into the NASDAQ chill of PacBell Park, or worse, new halls take big corporate bucks and leave us with the pathetic, Post-it poetry of the Staples Center—*proof* that Americans spend too much money on Sharpies.

I'm not fond of looking to the world of international soccer as a beacon of light and hope, but my hat's off to

them. I say we welcome Bargain Booze Stadium with open arms, and hope it ushers in a new era of naming rights.

And please note the word "Booze": not Spirits, not Liquor, not Aperitif Stadium. No elitist, Bombay Sapphire snoot. Nope, this fine municipal is a towering love letter to the fuel of tailgate parties from Orchard Park to Baton Rouge: BARGAIN BOOZE STADIUM. I can just see the faithful abbreviating it to "Good old B&B," "The house that ate me liver," "The palais de rotgut."

If we ever progress to this level stateside, we could name an entire American League's worth of cribs after the endless procession of cheap bourbons housed in plastic liters—the brands that sound like a pimply cousin of the good stuff. Case in point, you get the feeling J. T. S. Brown coulda been Jim Beam...if he'd just tried a little harder.

For the uninitiated, the language of bourbon comes in three varieties. Some are named after Southern gentlemen:

Jim Beam, George Dickel, or the lesser known brands...

Otis Q. Rotgut
Colonel Reflux
Ben Dover
Chuck M'dung
Don K. Balls
and T. J. Lush

Some cheap bourbon is named after a dear relative like Old Granddad, or the lesser known...

Crusty Old Gent
Professor Passblood
Kissin' Cousins
Cap'n Upchuck
And my favorite, Uncle Nose Vein

The final group is named after a mossy homestead, like Knob Creek, or the lesser known...

Tubercular Stream
Yellow Crick
Old Kentucky Mange
Incest Manor
Musty Mansion
And my favorite, Swill City

Now those are some stadium names a fan can relate to. Cheap bourbon—priced under twelve bucks, and guaranteed to strip the paint off an army tank, but it gets the job done. And as long as it still hurts, keep on sippin' until they finally relocate a major franchise to Kentucky.

The Winter X Games—renegade events created by pre-*Jackass* psychopathletes working with nothing more than a snowy hill, a stolen cafeteria tray, and plenty of Mother Nature. Can this counterculture jockapalooza really compare to the incumbent Winter Olympics? You better believe it, buddy. Now, let's see how they stack up at the Tale of the Tape.

WINTER X GAMES	WINTER OLYMPICS	
		INHERENT DANGERS: WINTER OLYMPICS: Terrorists WINTER X GAMES: Guys named Choady who keep shoving their skull-bongs at you and chanting, "Doooo it!"
-	-	ADVANTAGE: Push
		WHEN YOU WIN: WINTER OLYMPICS: You receive a medal as your national anthem plays. WINTER X GAMES: You scarf down a Cliff Bar as the P.A. blasts "Spread Your Love on Fly."
	X	ADVANTAGE: Olympics
		COULD LOSE... : WINTER OLYMPICS: Your event WINTER X GAMES: Your seventh vertebra
-	-	ADVANTAGE: Push
		BUT THEY DON'T TAKE: WINTER OLYMPICS: American Express WINTER X GAMES: Any crap from you
X		ADVANTAGE: X Games
		ORIGINATED AROUND THE TIME OF: WINTER OLYMPICS: Now-ancient Greece WINTER X GAMES: Now-ancient grunge
X		ADVANTAGE: X Games
		INTANGIBLES: WINTER OLYMPICS: Judges' scores can be compromised by bad will between nations. WINTER X GAMES: Judges' scores can be compromised by too much Xtasy (Why do you think they call them X Games?)
X		ADVANTAGE: X Games
		HASSLES FOR SPECTATORS: WINTER OLYMPICS: Long lines at Port-O-Sans WINTER X GAMES: Long lines at bushes
X		ADVANTAGE: X Games. Come on people, it's natural!
		HOST COUNTRY STOCKS VISITING ATHLETE'S FRIDGE WITH: WINTER X GAMES: Microbrews WINTER OLYMPICS: Yak blood smoothies
X		ADVANTAGE: X Games
		BIGGEST SELLING POINT: WINTER OLYMPICS: The thrill of victory and the agony of defeat WINTER X GAMES: No John Tesh!
X		ADVANTAGE: X Games
		WINNERS GO TO: WINTER OLYMPICS: The White House WINTER X GAMES: The Burning Man
X		ADVANTAGE: X Games
		FIRST PRIZE: WINTER OLYMPICS: Gold medals WINTER X GAMES: You get to live!
X		ADVANTAGE: X Games
		LIKELY ENDORSEMENTS FOR WINNERS: WINTER OLYMPICS: Breakfast cereal WINTER X GAMES: Disability insurance
	X	ADVANTAGE: Olympics
		MOTTO: WINTER OLYMPICS: Stronger, better, faster. WINTER X GAMES: Hey man, don't bogart that!
X		ADVANTAGE: X Games
		LIKELY TO NAME THEIR CHILDREN: WINTER OLYMPICS: Brendan and Parker WINTER X GAMES: Keirin and Rain
-	-	ADVANTAGE: Push, no winners here. And while we're on the subject, when did parents stop naming their kids "Joe"?

So there you have it; it's so simple when you break things down scientifically. In a half-pipe gravity-check face plant, the advantage goes to the Winter X Games. And why not? They deliver more skinned elbows than ever thought possible! Even on snow! All I can say is good luck, have a ball, and go easy on the clover cigarettes. Until next time, I'm Nick Bakay, reminding you the numbers never lie.

LUGE VS. STREET LUGE

I guess there are weirder things you can devote your life to than blindly hurtling, on your back, toward an unseen finish line. Showbiz for example…but nothing matches the commitment of this sport. Luge has expanded from a frozen Olympic sport to include its new, extreme brother, "street luge," which says it all. Luge, street luge, let's see how they stack up at the Tale of the Tape.

SURFACE:
LUGE: Ice
STREET LUGE: Asphalt
ADVANTAGE: Luge

NAGGING INJURIES:
LUGE: Frostbite
STREET LUGE: Gravel pants…think about it…
ADVANTAGE: Push…

WHAT YOU STEER WITH
LUGE: Your hips
STREET LUGE: Mr. Happy
ADVANTAGE: Street luge…

THE WINNER GETS:
LUGE: Pride, and the knowledge that you're the best
STREET LUGE: Thirty grand to pay for those skin grafts
ADVANTAGE: Street luge

FRICTION CAUSES
LUGE: Slower speeds
STREET LUGE: A slight, but not unpleasant, tingling sensation
ADVANTAGE: Street luge

HAZARDS:
LUGE: A dry patch in the ice
STREET LUGE: A stray Zagnut wrapper
ADVANTAGE: Push…

THE LAST THING THE ATHLETE WANTS TO HEAR:
LUGE: The Swede is leading by a millisecond!
STREET LUGE: Red light! Red light!
ADVANTAGE: Street Luge

GROUNDS FOR DISQUALIFICATION:
LUGE: False start
STREET LUGE: Skid marks
ADVANTAGE: Luge

GROUPIES ARE CALLED:
LUGE: Snow Cones
STREET LUGE: Curbside service
ADVANTAGE: Push…

THE DRIVER IS CALLED:
LUGE: Pilot
STREET LUGE: Keanu
ADVANTAGE: Luge

THE PRICE OF LOSING:
LUGE: There goes that Ricola endorsement
STREET LUGE: A private nurse swabbing your drool for the next forty years
ADVANTAGE: Luge

And finally:

THE ONLY THING STANDING BETWEEN THE LUGER AND AN ACCIDENT:
LUGE: The lane barrier
STREET LUGE: Flesh!
ADVANTAGE: Luge

So there you have it; it's so simple when you break things down scientifically. In a well-lubricated upset, the advantage goes to street luge! Ice luge, street luge, it can lead only to nude luge—coming soon to ESPN Blue. Until next time I'm Nick Bakay, reminding you the numbers never lie…

Mullets, Surfers, & Jackasses

Believe it or not, there was a time when a hairless dome was an express train to weirdville. Cue balls were the stuff of egghead scientists, psych ward escapees, and Lenin, the patron saint of all things un-American. Cut to today: Couldn't be cooler—provided you've got a skull that works with the aerodynamic look. It could be the upset of the ages, coiffure division. Now consider the humble mullet: oft derided, linked to hockey players, wrestlers, and hillbillies, never cool, but time will tell. I mean, if bald can conquer, anything is possible, and both are very much on display in the world of sports, from Michael Jordan's revolutionary bald to Barry Melrose's Hall of Fame mullet. Two extremes, one message: "Hey, look at me!" Let's see how they stack at the Tale of the Tape...

	MULLETS	SHAVED		
			BAD HAIR DAY:	
			SHAVED: I just nicked my brain!	
			MULLET: Someone asks you if the carnival is in town	
	X		ADVANTAGE: Mullet	
			NOT RECOMMENDED FOR:	
			SHAVED: Anyone with a knobby skull and neck cleavage	
			MULLET: Anyone applying for a MacArthur genius grant	
	-	-	ADVANTAGE: Push	

POSTER BOYS:
SHAVED: Michael Jordan, the championship years
MULLET: Billy Ray Cyrus, the "Achy Breaky Heart" years
X ADVANTAGE: Shaved

FOUNDING FATHERS:
SHAVED: Telly Savalas
MULLET: Pete Rose
- - ADVANTAGE: Push

GET READY TO BE CALLED:
SHAVED: Captain Picard
MULLET: The Boz
- - ADVANTAGE: Push

PRECAUTIONS:
SHAVED: Light can refract off cranium and reach laser-heat temps.
MULLET: Rat tail can snag in John Deere equipment.
- - ADVANTAGE: Push

CARE AND UPKEEP:
SHAVED: Lather, shave, blot
MULLET: Set Flobie to "Hayseed"
- - ADVANTAGE: Push

IT HELPS IF YOU HAVE:
SHAVED: A cut man in your corner
MULLET: Wranglers tight enough to visibly outline your urethra
- - ADVANTAGE: Push

AFFILIATED LEAGUES:
SHAVED: NBA, NFL, Blue Man Group
MULLET: NHL, WWE, Girl's Softball
X ADVANTAGE: Shaved

STATEMENTS MADE:
SHAVED: "I finally saw a photo of my comb-over."
MULLET: "I consider beer a food group."
X ADVANTAGE: Mullet

GIRLS THINK:

SHAVED: You're either a bouncer, or an android.

MULLET: You just got off work at the Tilt-A-Whirl.

ADVANTAGE: Push—either way it's another night with "Lefty."

SUBCULTURES YOU GET LUMPED IN WITH:

SHAVED: Hazing victims

MULLET: Lesbos

ADVANTAGE: Mullet—lesbos are red hot right now!

YOUR CLOSET IS FULL OF:

SHAVED: Head bandannas

MULLET: "Official Titty Inspector" T-shirts

ADVANTAGE: Push

MUSIC ICONS:

SHAVED: Sinead O'Connor

MULLET: Four out of five Oak Ridge Boys

ADVANTAGE: Push

DO THEY WORK IN WASHINGTON?:

SHAVED: Not for Jordan

MULLET: Not for Jagr

ADVANTAGE: Push

A GREAT WAY TO:

SHAVED: Discover a small but distinct "666" on your skull

MULLET: Cover that "Guns N' Roses Forever" tattoo on the back of your neck.

ADVANTAGE: Push

RESURRECTED BY THEIR COIFS:

SHAVED: Michael Chiklis

MULLET: Patrick Swayze

ADVANTAGE: Shaved

ON COLD NIGHTS:

SHAVED: Reach for your touk.

MULLET: Tie your hair around your ears.

ADVANTAGE: Push

FROM BEHIND, YOU LOOK LIKE:

SHAVED: A thumb

MULLET: Trisha Yearwood

ADVANTAGE: Mullet

MOTTOES:

SHAVED: Lex Luthor Rocks!

MULLET: Business in the front, party in the back.

ADVANTAGE: Mullet

A.K.A. :

SHAVED: Chrome Dome, Curly, Mr. Bigglesworth

MULLET: The Canadian Passport, Tennessee Top Hat, Beaver Paddle, Camaro Cut, Kentucky Waterfall, Missouri Compromise, Dirt Stick...

ADVANTAGE: Wow, I lost count. Let's move on...

A PRELUDE TO:

SHAVED: The relentless footsteps of your midlife crisis

MULLET: A shaved head

ADVANTAGE: Push

PRECLUDES:

SHAVED: A hat of ear hair

MULLET: Winning any legal battles

ADVANTAGE: Shaved

DEFLECTS ATTENTION FROM:

SHAVED: Bozo pattern baldness

MULLET: Gingivitis

ADVANTAGE: Shaved

So there you have it; it's all so simple when you break things down scientifically. In a quarter inch off the sides, the advantage goes to...the mullet! Talk about an upset, do you believe in miracles?! The bottom line is mullet or not, it's hair, baby, and as long as you've got hair, you've got the power. Ungowa. Until next time, I'm Nick Bakay, reminding you the numbers never lie.

Scripts be damned, nothing beats reality TV. Now I'm not talking about das uber reality of the Osbournes or supermodels purging larvae on *Fear Factor*; I'm talking the dodgy reality where danger lurks and people can get hurt. For my money, the country of reality is ruled by two kings: *The World's Strongest Man* and *Jackass*. One's cautious, one's reckless, but if either interrupts my channel surfing, I'm slack-jawed and slightly a-tingle. They diddle our reptilian brain, the one that *needs to see* muscular mutants don a yoke of swinging cement buckets and thrill-seeking slackers wade through alligator-infested swamps in raw-chicken underpants. As Aristotle once said, true drama must provoke fear and pity. I say, mission accomplished. *World's Strongest Man. Jackass.* Let's see how they stack up at the Tale of the Tape:

BODY TYPE:
WORLD'S STRONGEST MAN: Like a T-Rex in boy's briefs.
JACKASS: Bruised, inky man-a-bes
ADVANTAGE: Push

SUPPLEMENTS:
WORLD'S STRONGEST MAN: I'm gonna guess growth hormones harvested from the glands of oxen.
JACKASS: Nasally ingested earthworms
ADVANTAGE: *Jackass*

WARDROBE:
WORLD'S STRONGEST MAN: Tank tops, kneepads, jewelry
JACKASS: T-shirts from road-stand corn-dog joints, Chuck Taylors, live crawfish diapers
ADVANTAGE: *Jackass*

SIGNATURE EVENTS:
WORLD'S STRONGEST MAN: Dead lift, boat pull, Atlas stones
JACKASS: Whatever puts their plums in harm's way
ADVANTAGE: *World's Strongest Man*

RISKS:

WORLD'S STRONGEST MAN: Finding out you're only the world's *seventh* strongest man. Honorable mention: Say good-bye to the missionary position.

JACKASS: Really needing the wheelchair you're currently riding down a staircase

X **ADVANTAGE:** *Jackass*

SIDE EFFECTS:

WORLD'S STRONGEST MAN: Supplement-induced C cups

JACKASS: Wrongful death lawsuits

- - **ADVANTAGE:** Push

INHERENT DANGERS:

WORLD'S STRONGEST MAN: Halfway into your squat, you hear something snap "down there."

JACKASS: Your skateboard just impaled the cameraman.

X **ADVANTAGE:** *Jackass*

GROUPIES:

WORLD'S STRONGEST MAN: Yes, they're called "'Roid Riders."

JACKASS: The kind who write to imprisoned serial killers

X **ADVANTAGE:** *Jackass*

NICKNAMES:

WORLD'S STRONGEST MAN: The Prince of Prolapse, My Dinner with Andro, Enzyme, Stains, The Juice Man, Mr. Bump

JACKASS: Bam, Wee Man, Raab Himself, Hoofbite, and Johnny

X **ADVANTAGE:** *World's Strongest Man*

UNWITTING VICTIMS:

WORLD'S STRONGEST MAN: The beer kegs they heave over walls

JACKASS: Phil and April Margera

- - **ADVANTAGE:** Push

EARLY WARNING SIGNS IN YOUR OWN KID:

WORLD'S STRONGEST MAN: He lifts the minivan to retrieve an errant baseball.

JACKASS: He gets in his crib via a long leap from the top of a bookshelf.

- - **ADVANTAGE:** Push

(AND FOR MORE ON THIS SUBJECT, REFER TO OUR SPECIAL WARNING SIGNS ON PAGE 175.)

DISCLAIMER:
WORLD'S STRONGEST MAN: "The Federation is exempt from liability in the event of an injury."
JACKASS: "Do not try this at home."
ADVANTAGE: Push

PRE-GAME MEAL:
WORLD'S STRONGEST MAN: Smallest strong man in the competition
JACKASS: A snorted line of wasabi
X ADVANTAGE: *Jackass*

SUPPORT STAFF:
WORLD'S STRONGEST MAN: Coach, nutritionist, life partner
JACKASS: Medic, giant rubberband guy, entomologist
X ADVANTAGE: *Jackass*

DOUBLE JEOPARDY:
WORLD'S STRONGEST MAN: Pulling a tractor after choosing beans as your carb load-up
JACKASS: Wearing a suit of flap meat while playing with an attack dog
X ADVANTAGE: *Jackass*

WHAT THEY THINK OF EACH OTHER:
WORLD'S STRONGEST MAN: *Jackass*es are flecks of lint in the navel of mankind.
JACKASS: Looks like somebody's daddy didn't love him enough.
X ADVANTAGE: *Jackass*

FINGER ON THE PULSE OF:
WORLD'S STRONGEST MAN: The first Olympic games
JACKASS: My wife
X ADVANTAGE: *Jackass*. What can I say, Robin likes her bad boys.

MISCHIEF:
WORLD'S STRONGEST MAN: Loosening the lug nuts on the semi before the truck pull
JACKASS: Loosening the screws on Phil's desk chair
ADVANTAGE: Push

THE MOVIE:
WORLD'S STRONGEST MAN: Straight to streaming video
JACKASS: A $25 million opening weekend
X ADVANTAGE: *Jackass*

WHERE ELSE CAN YOU SEE?:
WORLD'S STRONGEST MAN: A half-naked man trembling as he hangs over a vat of water
JACKASS: A floor-sample toilet in need of a flush
X ADVANTAGE: *World's Strongest Man*

WHAT THE FUTURE HOLDS:
WORLD'S STRONGEST MAN: Skin reduction surgery after the muscle mass goes away
JACKASS: Evel Knievel status, and whatever's left from the dirty girl divorce
X ADVANTAGE: *Jackass*

FUTURE AILMENTS:
WORLD'S STRONGEST MAN: Kidneys that pump pure gasoline
JACKASS: Hip, coccyx, and scrotum replacement surgery
ADVANTAGE: Push

MODE OF TRANSPORTATION:
WORLD'S STRONGEST MAN: Why fly when you can pull the plane?
JACKASS: Pogo stick attached to stilts attached to a skateboard
X ADVANTAGE: *Jackass*

SOUNDS OF THE GAME:
WORLD'S STRONGEST MAN: Grunts, roars, pip-farts
JACKASS: Whimpers, Chippendales music, bulk laxatives at work
ADVANTAGE: Wow

Even if you delight in the *Jackass* crew's athlete/stuntman hybrid, you may worry that your kid wants to follow in their path. The dictionary defines "stunt" as "a display of skill or daring." A specialty stunt requires a little more than that—excruciating skill, unflinching discipline, and a very particular emotional constitution that shows up early in life. For any parents who think they may have a budding daredevil on their hands, here's a checklist...

WARNING SIGNS YOUR KID MIGHT GROW UP TO BE A *JACKASS*:

- There are fifteen smelly old mattresses piled outside your second-story bathroom window

- He names his dog "Kevlar."

- He thinks the stunt work in most movies is "too slick."

- He's the only kid in third grade who knows how to pull his punches

- He souped up his Big Wheel to go forty-five miles per hour

- You're on a first-name basis with the fire department

- When asked why his head is repeatedly submerged in the fish tank, he says he's training his gag reflex to handle live goldfish.

- That old Ford bumper? It's now a street luge

- Constructed a Ferris wheel out of old washing machines

- He often starts sentences with "Watch this!!!"

- The doctor has said the elbow skin will never grow back.

So there you have it; it's all so easy when you break it down scientifically. In a jury-rigged vert-ramp straight to the stars, the advantage goes to *Jackass*. Sorry, big men, we all know you can pull a semi, but big deal—Johnny Knoxville returned kicks with no blockers against the USC Trojans, dressed in a Tennessee Volunteers uniform! Now that's a man. Until next time, I'm Nick Bakay, reminding you that the numbers never lie.

If the NHL wants to raise the profile of hockey, I say sell America on the sheer anarchy of play-off hockey violence—that special time of the hockey year when teeth spill over the ice like a spilled box of Chiclets. Think about it—it's the only marketing pocket left for hockey. The NBA is synonymous with urban, NASCAR owns country, and the NFL and MLB have divvied up the middle class.

I say: Go badass. This is a strange game that most Americans have never played. But we can relate to a series of jabs to the nose. Violence sells in this millennium.

How else do you explain the single greatest marketing miracle of the last decade, the WWE? And their fights aren't even real! These "games" have more in common than you might think, but is it really that simple? Pro hockey, pro wrestling, let's see how they stack up at the Tale of the Tape...

FIGHTS:
WWE: Fake
NHL: Real
ADVANTAGE: NHL

SHOULDERS:
WWE: Real
NHL: Fake
ADVANTAGE: WWE

FACE-OFF:
WWE: A result
NHL: A start
ADVANTAGE: NHL

HOW TO BE AN ALL-STAR:
WWE: Have a working tail surgically implanted
NHL: Get traded to Detroit
ADVANTAGE: WWE

MOST DANGEROUS PLACE TO BE:
WWE: Guarding the supplement cabinet
NHL: In front of the net
ADVANTAGE: Push

GOUGE:
WWE: A way to attack your opponents eyeball
NHL: A way to describe ticket pricing
ADVANTAGE: WWE

WHERE ELSE CAN YOU SEE?:
WWE: Men spending long periods of time with their heads squeezed by another man's buttocks
NHL: Twelve men on the ice, three teeth
ADVANTAGE: Push

COLORFUL CHARACTERS:
WWE: Mr. Vince McMahon
NHL: The organist who underscores a penalty by playing the theme from *Dragnet*
ADVANTAGE: WWE

WHEN YOU'RE BAD, YOU:
WWE: Take a folding chair to the lumbar region.
NHL: Spend five minutes in the penalty box and think about who to pummel when you get back out there.
ADVANTAGE: NHL

MARKED CHARACTERISTICS:
WWE: Quivering, greased man-flanks
NHL: More facial scars than the entire Jackson family
ADVANTAGE: WWE

HOW TO TELL WHEN A GUY HAS BEEN HIT HARD:
WWE: The guy hitting him stomps on the canvas *extra*-loud.
NHL: He *don't* get up.
ADVANTAGE: NHL

WHERE THE SPORTS WERE BORN:
WWE: At the corner of Sadist Street and Latent Blvd.
NHL: A pond
ADVANTAGE: NHL

MOST EXCITING MOMENT:
WWE: A cage match with an electric fence
NHL: A penalty shot with a bouncing puck
ADVANTAGE: WWE

DULLEST MOMENT:
WWE: When the fans trail into the arena, leaving a wake of drool
NHL: Icing
ADVANTAGE: NHL

WHY SOME OF THEM WEAR MASKS:
WWE: To hide their identity until they can think up a new character
NHL: So they can also play goalie in Mexico
ADVANTAGE: Push

WORLD'S LARGEST SOURCE OF:
WWE: 270-pound men with peroxide-blond hair
NHL: Male rhinoplasty
ADVANTAGE: NHL

JANITORIAL:
WWE: A transient squeegees off the mat.
NHL: A trainer hits the bench with a can of Loogie-Be-Gone.
ADVANTAGE: Push

FRANCHISES THAT HAVE YET TO TAKE OFF:
WWE: Stone Cold Steve Austin's World of Unfinished Pine Furniture
NHL: Jaromir Jagr's House of Late-Seventies Hair
ADVANTAGE: NHL, representin' mullets everywhere

COMING SOON TO A STORE NEAR YOU:
WWE: Crime scene clean-up kit
NHL: It's not just any tongue scraper—it's a Ziggy Palffy!
ADVANTAGE: NHL

THE REF LOOKS THE OTHER WAY:
WWE: When a wrestler sneaks a foreign object in the ring
NHL: When Brett Hull scores the final goal of the season
ADVANTAGE: WWE, and don't let them tell you I keep hammering this home because I'm from Buffalo. Can you put a qualifier on justice?

So there you have it; in a triple-suplex during four-on-four O.T., the advantage goes...to the WWE. But if the NHL was taking notes, this country will have a Zamboni in every garage. Until next time, I'm Nick Bakay, reminding you the numbers never lie.

TRADE
WRITING

Baseball deals rarely get done without gun-to-the-head pressure. Much is made of valiant GMs furiously working the phones and filing contracts before midnight.

On the other hand, sportswriters have another word for deadlines—daily! Miss one, and your readers get to enjoy their morning Maypo with some expanded box scores and a bonus Tank McNamara. But when it comes to working with a ticking clock, who has the rougher ride? GMs, sportswriters, both push the envelope—let's see how they stack up at the Tale of the Tape...

BIGGEST DISTRACTION:
GM: Sportswriters
SPORTSWRITER: Bourbon
X ADVANTAGE: Sportswriter

DAMAGED GOODS:
GM: You closed a deal for a proven starter, and an AA prospect who died last summer in a cotton candy machine mishap.
SPORTSWRITER: The kind of women you meet while faxing in a Kinko's at 4 A.M.
X ADVANTAGE: Sportswriter. To quote Woody Allen, "The heart wants what the heart wants."

UH-OH:
GM: You acquire a player who fathered three children with your owner's wife.
SPORTSWRITER: Your editor discovers that your team "insider" is actually Toby, the mentally challenged towel boy.
- - ADVANTAGE: Push

FUTURE CONSIDERATIONS:
GM: A fancy way of saying, "Three cases of groin ointment"
SPORTSWRITER: What you must face when you use your column to nickname a player "Captain Over-the-Hill," *then* need him for some clubhouse quotes
- - ADVANTAGE: Push

MASSAGING THE TRUTH:
GM: "You won't just be signing a contract, you'll be joining the entire Devil Rays family..."
SPORTSWRITER: "Don't worry, Mr. Rocker, this is off the record."
X ADVANTAGE: Sportswriter

BIGGEST HEADACHE:
GM: Making Barry Bonds a multiyear offer without paying the luxury tax
SPORTSWRITER: Making Barry Bonds remotely sympathetic
X ADVANTAGE: GM

COMMAND FROM BOSS:
GM: "We need a front-line starter, a second baseman, and a lower payroll."
SPORTSWRITER: "Three hundred words on ice dancing, and it better be punchy."
- - ADVANTAGE: Push

DREAM PHONE CALL:
GM: "Hi, this is Alex Rodriguez. Any chance I could sign for the minimum?"
SPORTSWRITER: "I am Anna Kournikova. You come interview me—in my apartment. Yes?"
X ADVANTAGE: Sportswriter

ICHIRO:
GM: The find of the year
SPORTSWRITER: "For the love of God, does anyone speak Japanese?"
X ADVANTAGE: GM

DISASTERS:
GM: *What*, no trade clause?!
SPORTSWRITER: You just spilled nacho cheese sauce on your modem.
ADVANTAGE: Push

COMPLICATIONS:
GM: Closing a last-minute deal with a GM who stutters
SPORTSWRITER: You're still drunk from last night.
X ADVANTAGE: Sportswriter

LEGALESE:
GM: Your new closer's rap lyrics have been subpoenaed.
SPORTSWRITER: Your proofreader is still busy studying for his citizenship test.
X ADVANTAGE: Sportswriter, and freedom, baby!

BEWARE OF:
GM: Mileage on the cadaver tendon in your new star's pitching arm
SPORTSWRITER: Hallucinating from bad press-box sushi
ADVANTAGE: Push

FISCAL FOLLIES:
GM: Your owner is so cheap he makes you dial 10-10-2-20 before every call.
SPORTSWRITER: You tried to charge dinner at The Palm to your expense account.
ADVANTAGE: Push

BAD NEWS:
GM: Your phone is bugged by Scott Boras.
SPORTSWRITER: "S" key breaks during Sammy Sosa article.
ADVANTAGE: Push

TEN MINUTES TO GO:
GM: "We need to seal this. Toss in a cheerleader."
SPORTSWRITER: "Quick, I need a verb."
X ADVANTAGE: GM

ON THE LINE:
GM: Millions of dollars
SPORTSWRITER: Dozens of dollars
X ADVANTAGE: GM

ASSISTANT:
GM: A motivated Ivy League graduate
SPORTSWRITER: Smokes, NoDoz, Nicorette gum
X ADVANTAGE: Sportswriter

ULTIMATE GOAL:
GM: A world championship
SPORTSWRITER: Comedy column on ESPN.COM
ADVANTAGE: Push

Okay, I may have reached on that last one, but there you have it. This one may have had more pushes than Sumo, but it's all so simple when you break things down scientifically. In a player to be named later, the advantage goes to sportswriters. Allow me to alert the media! Until next time, I'm Nick Bakay, reminding you the numbers never lie.

SPORTS MOVIES

BLAXPLOITATION MOVIES

As far as I'm concerned, sports movies get more credit than they deserve. There are a handful of great ones, but the genre is hamstrung by the constant regurgitation of two plots: A rag-tag team learns how to work together, and against colossal odds wins the big game. Or, an individual athlete can't conquer his inner demons until an unlikely source teaches him a life lesson, and he realizes that sometimes you have to lose in order to win. It's formulaic, predictable, never quite as good as watching an actual game—especially when an elite athlete is portrayed by Anthony Perkins. Now, if you're looking for an underappreciated genre, try the classic blaxploitation films of the seventies. Oh sure, they may be retro groovy now, but back in the day I stood in the ticket line for *Superfly* four times. Oscars for *Rocky*, but not for *Cleopatra Jones*? Let's see how they stack up at the Tale of the Tape...

WHAT YOU HAVE TO BUY INTO:
BLAXPLOITATION: Rudy Ray Moore is good at karate.
SPORTS MOVIE: A professional actor can bat convincingly from the left side of the plate.
ADVANTAGE: Push

THE GREAT ONES:
BLAXPLOITATION: *Superfly*
SPORTS MOVIE: *Rocky*
ADVANTAGE: Push

SWING AND A MISS:
BLAXPLOITATION: *Superfly TNT*
SPORTS MOVIE: *Rocky 24*
ADVANTAGE: Push

UNDERRATED:
BLAXPLOITATION: *Willie Dynamite*
SPORTS MOVIE: *North Dallas Forty*
ADVANTAGE: Sports

OVERRATED:
BLAXPLOITATION: *The Mack*
SPORTS MOVIE: *The Natural*
ADVANTAGE: Blaxploitation

Nick Bakay's Tale of the Tape

POSTER ART:
BLAXPLOITATION: A ghetto-fabulous player, legs akimbo, with a girl hugging one and a gun hugging the other
SPORTS MOVIE: Airbrushed Keanu among airbrushed inner city kids
X ADVANTAGE: Blaxploitation—this stuff was *meant* to be painted on velvet.

LOG LINES:
BLAXPLOITATION: "The mob put the finger on Slaughter, so he gave them the finger right back... curled around a trigger!" (*Slaughter's Big Rip-off*)
SPORTS MOVIE: "If you believe the impossible, the incredible can come true" (*Field of Dreams*). Geh?
X ADVANTAGE: Blaxploitation

TRAILER MUSIC:
BLAXPLOITATION: Phlanged wah-wah
SPORTS MOVIE: "Put Me in, Coach!"
X ADVANTAGE: Nothing against John Fogerty, but survey says wah-wah.

THE ENEMY:
BLAXPLOITATION: "The Man"
SPORTS MOVIE: Mitch Gaylord's acting
X ADVANTAGE: Blaxploitation

CLASSIC DIALOGUE:
BLAXPLOITATION: "Yo bitch, I said where my blow at?!"
SPORTS MOVIE: "Uh, Phil...you *do* speak Canadian, don't you?"
– – ADVANTAGE: Push

SONGS THAT CARRIED BAD MOVIES:
BLAXPLOITATION: *Chariots of Fire*
SPORTS MOVIE: *Shaft*
X ADVANTAGE: *Shaft*—still a waaay better movie than a pretentious hunk o' snoot about pale men running. Screen it today and tell me I'm wrong.

FEMALE ICONS:
BLAXPLOITATION: Pam Grier
SPORTS MOVIE: Mariel Hemingway
X ADVANTAGE: Blaxploitation

WHEN GENRES COLLIDE:
BLAXPLOITATION: *Black Belt Jones*
SPORTS MOVIE: *The Split*
X ADVANTAGE: Blaxploitation

WARDROBE:
BLAXPLOITATION: More crushed velvet than a million 70s prom tuxedos.
SPORTS MOVIE: None in the de rigueur whirlpool scene.
– – ADVANTAGE: Push

ACCESSORIES:
BLAXPLOITATION: Felt lid, coke spoon necklace, platforms, purple fur wrap
SPORTS MOVIE: Um...his lucky bat?
X ADVANTAGE: Blaxploitation

HOW DID WE LET THINGS GO THIS FAR?:
BLAXPLOITATION: *Disco Godfather*
SPORTS MOVIE: *Major League 5*
X ADVANTAGE: Blaxploitation, on bombast alone.

So there you have it; it's all so simple when you break things down scientifically. The big payback, and the advantage, goes to blaxploitation movies. No surprises here. If we've learned anything today, it's the simple fact that "ain't no one crosses Willie Dynamite. He's tight, together and mean. Chicks, chumps, he uses 'em all. He's got to be #1," but he still doesn't have an NHL franchise named after him. Until next time, I'm Nick Bakay, reminding you the numbers never lie.

In Los Angeles, getting to the airport is considered a motor sport. It's got the pressure, the pit stops, and the inevitable wild card of lane closures. Unfortunately, rather than kudos and cash, the prize for racing to LAX on the San Diego Freeway is a week with the father-in-law and his wife. Not exactly Formula One racing, but with a little imagination and a helmet, well, a man can ignore his mocking wife and dream, can't he? Still, which is more thrilling—Formula One, or a white-knuckle race to pick up the arriving father-in-law? Let's see how they stack up at the Tale of the Tape...

	FORMULA ONE	FATHER-IN-LAW	

RAISON D'ÊTRE:
FORMULA ONE RACING: To win
PICKING UP FATHER-IN-LAW: Hoping your wife acquiesces on your birthday this year
| | | X | ADVANTAGE: Father-in-law. Hope springs eternal.

VEHICLES:
FORMULA ONE RACING: 3-litre V10 with maximum RPM not to exceed 18,000
PICKING UP FATHER-IN-LAW: Blacked-out Caddy STS
| | | X | ADVANTAGE: Father-in-law. Not to exceed 18,000—feh.

MPH:
FORMULA ONE RACING: Approximately 225
PICKING UP FATHER-IN-LAW: About 5
| | X | | ADVANTAGE: Formula One

PROTECTIVE GEAR:
FORMULA ONE RACING: Kevlar suits, helmets, gloves
PICKING UP FATHER-IN-LAW: A fake smile and the pink glow of a breakfast Bloody
| | X | | ADVANTAGE: Formula One. You look like a superhero.

TRAFFIC:
FORMULA ONE RACING: Andretti's grandson is drafting your wake.
PICKING UP FATHER-IN-LAW: Trapped behind a minivan whose turn signal has been blinking for the last five miles.
| | X | | ADVANTAGE: Formula One

TO PASS TIME:
FORMULA ONE RACING: Count the times you can recite all the lyrics to "American Pie" before the end of the race.
PICKING UP FATHER-IN-LAW: Curse the SUVs blocking your view of the accident site.
| | | X | ADVANTAGE: Father-in-law

NOT SO GOOD:
FORMULA ONE RACING: S-turns in the rain
PICKING UP FATHER-IN-LAW: Dog vomit in the backseat
| | | X | ADVANTAGE: Father-in-law

CHALLENGES:
FORMULA ONE RACING: Looking cool on a gurney in a neck brace
PICKING UP FATHER-IN-LAW: Finding a parking space
| | | X | ADVANTAGE: Father-in-law

VICTORY:
FORMULA ONE RACING: The warm tingle at the sight of the waving flag
PICKING UP FATHER-IN-LAW: The cold sweat of spotting him in baggage claim
| | X | | ADVANTAGE: Formula One

EXTRAS:
FORMULA ONE RACING: Fame and fortune
PICKING UP FATHER-IN-LAW: Six days with someone bound to lose his hearing aid. Again.
| | X | | ADVANTAGE: Formula One

REASONS FOR YOUR SLOW START:
FORMULA ONE RACING: Fuel pump sludge
PICKING UP FATHER-IN-LAW: Malaise, dread, and trying to locate the Zantac
| | | X | ADVANTAGE: Father-in-law. Chances are, emotions won't cause a fiery death.

PAINTED IN REARVIEW MIRROR:

FORMULA ONE RACING: The new guy gaining on you

PICKING UP FATHER-IN-LAW: The old guy still pissed you're banging his daughter

X ADVANTAGE: Father-in-law

MISTAKES:

FORMULA ONE RACING: "Oh, I thought that was lap 76..."

PICKING UP FATHER-IN-LAW: Convincing his wife that it's "fajita," not "*fra*-geeta."

X ADVANTAGE: Father-in-law. A laugh is a laugh, even if you have to wait till they leave.

JUNK IN THE TRUNK:

FORMULA ONE RACING: No trunk, no junk

PICKING UP FATHER-IN-LAW: Many bags, none containing gifts

X ADVANTAGE: Formula One

PEOPLE WHO MIGHT WANDER INTO YOUR PATH:

FORMULA ONE RACING: Papparazzi

PICKING UP FATHER-IN-LAW: Someone selling oranges

X ADVANTAGE: Formula One

PRIZE:

FORMULA ONE RACING: Money, respect of your peers

PICKING UP FATHER-IN-LAW: They unpack in your bedroom.

X ADVANTAGE: Formula One

CHECKERED FLAG:

FORMULA ONE RACING: Winner!

PICKING UP FATHER-IN-LAW: The old man's new swim trunks

X ADVANTAGE: Father-in-law. His old trunks were covered with "You know you're a redneck when..." sayings.

EYES FIXED:

FORMULA ONE RACING: On the steely focus of victory

PICKING UP FATHER-IN-LAW: On the bloody, droopy-eye thing the old man's got going

X ADVANTAGE: Formula One

MONOTONY:

FORMULA ONE RACING: The endless shifting of gears

PICKING UP FATHER-IN-LAW: The endless smiling for his wife's camera

X ADVANTAGE: Formula One

THE PRICE YOU PAY:

FORMULA ONE RACING: Perhaps your legs?

PICKING UP FATHER-IN-LAW: 168 hours you'll never get back

-- ADVANTAGE: Push

STRESS MEANS:

FORMULA ONE RACING: Reabsorbing the adrenaline

PICKING UP FATHER-IN-LAW: You have to repeat the race next Saturday and nail the 8 A.M. departure.

X ADVANTAGE: Father-in-law

DIN:

FORMULA ONE RACING: The deafening roar of the engines

PICKING UP FATHER-IN-LAW: Increases with his incessant alcohol intake

X ADVANTAGE: Formula One

So there you have it; it's all so simple when you break things down scientifically. In a computerized active suspension system, the advantage goes to Formula One. But don't worry, George. At least I never asked you for a loan. Until next time, I'm Nick Bakay, reminding you that the numbers never lie.

SURFERS VS. THE EMPLOYED

Surfers—unemployed bums who refuse to let John Q. Establishment stick them in four-by-four boxes, or simply free spirits? And how do they match up against the tax-paying worker bees? Let's see how they stack up at the Tale of the Tape.

TYPICAL NAMES:
THE EMPLOYED: Bob Johnson
SURFERS: Choady
X | ADVANTAGE: The employed

OFTEN HEARD:
THE EMPLOYED: Hold my calls.
SURFERS: Duuude!
- - | ADVANTAGE: Push

PULLING OUT:
SURFERS: How you avoid crashing off a wave
THE EMPLOYED: How you avoid that third kid
X | ADVANTAGE: Surfers

KEEPING AN EYE OUT FOR:
SURFERS: The perfect wave
THE EMPLOYED: Disgruntled coworkers
X | ADVANTAGE: Surfer

MOTTOES:
THE EMPLOYED: Another day, another dollar
SURFERS: Huh?
X | ADVANTAGE: The employed

WOMEN SEE THEM AS:
SURFERS: A summer fling
THE EMPLOYED: A husband they can ride like a rented mule
X | ADVANTAGE: Surfers

POWER BREAKFASTS:
THE EMPLOYED: Grape-Nuts and high blood pressure medication
SURFERS: Whatever your mom has in the fridge
X | ADVANTAGE: Surfers

BAD DAYS:
THE EMPLOYED: An efficiency expert eliminates your job.
SURFERS: A shark eliminates your tibia.
X | ADVANTAGE: The employed

WHERE DOES IT GET YOU?:
THE EMPLOYED: Slowly ground down under the merciless heel of industry.
SURFERS: You wake up one morning, you're forty-eight years old, and you still think an IRA is a bunch of pissed-off Irishmen.
- - | ADVANTAGE: Push

A TUBE RIDE:
SURFERS: Catching a wave
THE EMPLOYED: You know...
X | ADVANTAGE: The employed

So there you have it; in a closed-due-to-rip-tides day at the beach, the advantage goes to Push. But hang in there, surfer dudes, *Blue Crush* is sure to gain you some mainstream respect. Oh, it didn't? Oh well...Until next time, I'm Nick Bakay, reminding you the numbers never lie.

NHL VS. NBA

The NBA remains a juggernaut of sorts, while the NHL lusts for Arena Football's ratings. Different as their urban and arctic roots may be, both have nets, refs, and share the twenty-thousand-seat auditoriums that remind me of the heavy-metal triple-bills of my youth: Blue Öyster Cult–UFO–Nazareth—I don't even remember the third encore! But, who's got the better game? Gary Bettman is the only suit who's worked both sides of that buffet, the rest of us have to use our puzzlers. Hoops. Pucks. Let's see how they stack up at the Tale of the Tape...

NHL NBA

LEAST EXCITING PLAY:		**HOW THEY SETTLE DISPUTES:**
NBA: The first forty-six minutes		NBA: A jump ball
NHL: Icing		NHL: A jump face
X	ADVANTAGE: NBA	X	ADVANTAGE: NHL

Nick Bakay's Tale of the Tape

TRIBAL WAR PAINT:
NBA: Allen Iverson's homophobic tattoos
NHL: Goalie mask painted to resemble Allen Iverson
ADVANTAGE: NBA

SUPERSTARS IN ACTION:
NBA: Kobe wide open, creating magic...
NHL: Forsberg crossing the blue line with four guys carving his shins into leg tartare. It's like Steve McQueen in *The Great Escape*—you know they're going to bring him down before he reaches the border.
ADVANTAGE: NBA

FAN INTERACTION:
NBA: Wave those squiggly things to distract the shooter at the foul line.
NHL: Heave a squid!
ADVANTAGE: NHL

DANGEROUS WORKING CONDITIONS:
NBA: The floor is slick with sweat.
NHL: The ice is coagulating.
ADVANTAGE: Push. Kids: Nobody wins with bodily fluids...

AGGRESSIVE MOVES:
NBA: Penetrate the lane
NHL: Penetrate Karya with your Koho...
ADVANTAGE: NBA

WHICH ESPN STUDIO ANALYST WOULD WIN IN A STREET FIGHT:
NBA: Dr. Jack Ramsay
NHL: Barry Melrose
ADVANTAGE: The NHL! It's not even close and that hurts. I was a Buffalo Braves fan back when Dr. Jack coached 'em, and if you're thinking to yourself, "Ernie No-D," you can kiss my ass.

PLAYER-FAN RELATIONS:
NBA: $1,000 a seat to see Calvin Klein "sharing" with Latrelle
NHL: A fraction of that price to watch an enforcer climb the glass and pummel a drunk lawyer
ADVANTAGE: NHL...

OFFICIATING:
NBA: Never call traveling on a superstar.
NHL: Never call a penalty in the third period.
ADVANTAGE: Push

MAN IN THE CREASE:
NBA: How most NBA stars relax
NHL: How Dallas won the cup
ADVANTAGE: NBA

TOTAL ENTERTAINMENT:
NBA: Those wacky, trampoline-dunkin' mascots!
NHL: That incredible moment when the Zamboni cleans the last patch of ice!
ADVANTAGE: NHL!

So there you have it; it's so simple when you break things down scientifically. In a penalty-shot buzzer-beater, the advantage goes to the NHL! But hang in there, NBA; at least Americans under*stand* your rules. Until next time, I'm Nick Bakay, reminding you the numbers never lie.

DOWNHILL SKIING VS. CROSS-COUNTRY SKIING

DOWNHILL

CROSS-COUNTRY

The gentle lift of a cold T-bar on your frozen bum-cakes, or the quiet shushing through a winter wonderland—two winter sports so similar, yet so very different. The torture of cross-country skiing vs. the glamorous flight of downhill skiing. A quick burst of speed vs. a race that lasts longer than a Tommy Lasorda sound bite. Cross-country, downhill—let's see how they stack up at the Tale of the Tape...

EQUIPMENT:
DOWNHILL: Long, stiff skis
CROSS-COUNTRY: Short and flexible skis
X ADVANTAGE: Long, stiff ones

TRAINING:
DOWNHILL: Pushing the envelope on the steepest slopes
CROSS-COUNTRY: Walking as fast as I can!
X ADVANTAGE: Downhill

FINISH LINE THEATRICS:
DOWNHILL: Raise arms, sip champagne.
CROSS-COUNTRY: Weep, then vomit.
X ADVANTAGE: Downhill

ENDORSEMENTS:
DOWNHILL: Tommy Moe for Snickers
CROSS-COUNTRY: Gunde Svan for boiled woolen clogs
X ADVANTAGE: Cross-country!

NAME MEANS:
DOWNHILL: Picabo Street: shining water
CROSS-COUNTRY: Marjut Lukkarinen: yellow snow!
X ADVANTAGE: Cross-country! I smell controversy...

KEYS TO WINNING:
DOWNHILL: Hugging the gates
CROSS-COUNTRY: Blood doping
X ADVANTAGE: Downhill

THE IDEAL BODY TYPE:
DOWNHILL: Shaped like a pear, heavily muscled in the thighs and buttocks
CROSS-COUNTRY: Shaped like a Slim Jim, like Jimmie "Dy-no-mite" Walker
X ADVANTAGE: Cross-country. Dy-no-mite indeed!

AERODYNAMICS:
DOWNHILL: A classic tuck to cut wind
CROSS-COUNTRY: Tall and fluid, to break wind
- - ADVANTAGE: Push—there are no winners here.

FANS:
DOWNHILL: Screaming drunks with cowbells
CROSS-COUNTRY: Trolls and odd mountain folk
X ADVANTAGE: Cross-country

INSPIRED BY:
DOWNHILL: Man's obsession with speed
CROSS-COUNTRY: Norway's love affair with leg cramps
X ADVANTAGE: Downhill

GROUPIES:
DOWNHILL: All those Bunny-Hill Annies
CROSS-COUNTRY: All the sin a man can muster above the timberline
X ADVANTAGE: Cross-country, in a shocker. Chock one up for small woodland creatures.

INNER MONOLOGUE:

DOWNHILL: "Stay low and don't panic."

CROSS-COUNTRY: "Give me a break, give me a break, break me off a piece of dat Keet Kat Bar."

X ADVANTAGE: Cross-country.

INCENTIVES:

DOWNHILL: Thousands of dollars in glamour-sport endorsements

CROSS-COUNTRY: A bottomless wheel of billy goat cheese

X ADVANTAGE: Downhill

WHAT YOU HAVE TO LOOK FORWARD TO:

DOWNHILL: Two minutes of pure adrenaline

CROSS-COUNTRY: The fortieth kilometer, when your body reaches ketosis and starts digesting itself...

X ADVANTAGE: Downhill

THE WORST THAT COULD HAPPEN:

DOWNHILL: You wipe out and become the new Agony of Defeat guy.

CROSS-COUNTRY: You live, and have to finish the race.

– – ADVANTAGE: Push—there are no winners here.

So there you have it; it's so simple when you break things down scientifically. In an avalanche, the advantage goes to downhill skiing. Well, it figures, the rich get richer and most downhillers have nary a school-loan payment among them. But don't hurt for cross-country skiers, they're still number one with the Ricola guys. Until next time, I'm Nick Bakay, reminding you the numbers never lie.

ATHLETES
WRITERS

Wazzup with college football rankings being decided by sportswriters? Sort of like closing your eyes and trying to guess who would win, Bigfoot or Batman? How whimsical... There has to be a better way. Like maybe the players should decide it on the playing field? BCS and no play-off system be damned, I say we put them to the test...college football players, college sportswriters, let's see how they stack up at the Tale of the Tape...

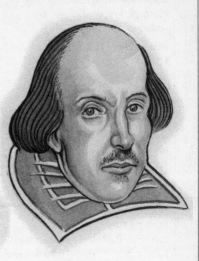

AVERAGE HEIGHT:
ATHLETES: 6' 2"
WRITERS: 5' 5"
ADVANTAGE: Athletes

AVERAGE WEIGHT:
ATHLETES: A sculpted 250
WRITERS: A nougatty 240
ADVANTAGE: Athletes

PREGAME RITUAL:
ATHLETES: Tape the left ankle first, then the right ankle.
WRITERS: Sober up.
ADVANTAGE: Push...

GAME DAY UNIFORM DECISIONS:
ATHLETES: Turf cleats or grass cleats?
WRITERS: Can I get another day out of these underpants?
ADVANTAGE: Athletes

Nick Bakay's Tale of the Tape

X

NEXT MOVE:
ATHLETES: Get lured away by big money and turn pro after junior year.
WRITERS: Get lured away by big offer from *Penny Saver*.
ADVANTAGE: Athletes

X

QUALIFICATIONS:
ATHLETES: The three T's: talent, toughness, tenacity
WRITERS: A pencil
ADVANTAGE: Athletes

X

SALARIES:
ATHLETES: Free education, Corvette, a job for Aunt Millie, and some luggage
WRITERS: $32,500 and unlimited clubhouse cold cuts
ADVANTAGE: Athletes

INTRODUCTION:
ATHLETES: Now starting at quarterback, Eli Manning.
WRITERS: My name is John, and I'm an alcoholic.

X

ADVANTAGE: Okay, cheap shot goes to the writers.

X

OCCUPATIONAL HAZARDS:
ATHLETES: Popping an anterior cruciate ligament
WRITERS: Spilling instant coffee on your keyboard
ADVANTAGE: Writers

X

IDENTIFICATION:
WRITERS: Press credentials
ATHLETES: Fraternity brand
ADVANTAGE: Writers...unless you've got that Ponderosa cattle brand on your biceps; that's just cool.

LITERARY IRONY:
ATHLETES: Can't read your diploma.
WRITERS: Devoted their lives to writing about illiterates.

- -

ADVANTAGE: Push—there are no winners here.

So there you have it; when we tally it up, the advantage goes to the players, which in turn is a strong vote for a play-off system in college football. But until things change, the pen is mightier than the sword. Ah, let the scribes have one last moment of power before the kids turn pro and nail them with that Bret Saberhagen bleach gun. Until next time, I'm Nick Bakay, reminding you that regardless of the BCS or the writer's poll, Mike Lupica's still really short.